"Michelle Long has created a very [...] anyone considering starting a QuickB[...] Her use of real-life examples and the [...] [...] [...] [...] [...] used her own experiences along with those of other leading QuickBooks Consultants is very compelling."

Alison Ball
Senior Program Manager, Accountant Training Network
Intuit Inc.

"Sharing best practices is what Michelle Long does best - whether it's teaching QuickBooks in the classroom or sharing her tips in this comprehensive guide to building a successful QuickBooks consulting business. And the best part is: Michelle actually practices what she preaches - in her own consulting business. Michelle's guide is full of practical how-to's and is the perfect first step for anyone contemplating starting a Quick-Books consulting business."

Cheri Streeter, MBA
Small Business Development Center Director
Overland Park, KS

"Michelle's book gives so much useful information. I only wish it was available when I started my practice years ago."

Liz Alexander, CPA
Member Intuit Certified Trainer Network
Advanced Certified QuickBooks ProAdvisor

"The best way to prepare yourself for a rewarding career, is to do your homework (read about, survey and learn from others) this book is all of that...."

Dawn Scranton
Accounting Directors, Inc.
Advanced Certified QuickBooks ProAdvisor

Successful
QuickBooks
Consulting

The Comprehensive Guide to
Starting and Growing a
QuickBooks Consulting Business

Michelle L. Long, CPA, MBA

Successful QuickBooks Consulting

Author: Michelle L. Long, CPA, MBA

Editor: Cheri Streeter, MBA

Publisher: CreateSpace Publishing, Scotts Valley, CA

Cover: Entrepreneur Advertising Group, LLC

Printed in the United States of America

ISBN: 1434810690

EAN-13: 9781434810694

Author: mlong@mlongconsulting.com or www.mlongconsulting.com.
Please email me your comments or suggestions for future editions.

Disclaimer/Limitation of Liability

This book is designed to provide accurate and authoritative information about the subject matter covered. It is sold with the understanding that the publisher and author are not rendering legal, accounting, or other professional advice. If such professional advice is needed, then the services of a competent professional should be sought.

While efforts have been made to ensure the accuracy and completeness of the information provided in this book, there may be typographical mistakes and/or mistakes in content. Therefore, this book should be used only as a guide and not as the only source of information of the subject matter covered.

The purpose of this book is to educate and provide information and resources about the subject matter covered. The author specifically disclaims all warranties or any liability or responsibility to any person or entity with respect to any loss or damage caused or alleged to be caused directly or indirectly by the information contained in this book. The fact that a company, organization, or website is mentioned in this book as a resource for further information does not mean that the author endorses the information, products or services provided by the resource. The resources mentioned should be researched and evaluated by the reader and the author is not liable for any information, content provided by those resources mentioned

If you do not wish to be bound by the above, you may return this book to the publisher for a full refund.

Foreword

In Stephen Covey's highly acclaimed book, *The 7 Habits of Highly Effective People*, he defines Habit 2 as "Begin with the End in Mind." Later in his expanded discussion of this concept, he states, "The extent to which you begin with the end in mind often determines whether or not you are able to create a successful enterprise. Most business failures begin in the first creation, with problems such as undercapitalization, misunderstanding of the market, or lack of a business plan." In this comprehensive guide to building a successful business (that just happens to be specific to QuickBooks consulting), Michelle Long embraces this principle defined by Covey back in 1989.

In her concise, conversational tone, Michelle guides the prospective consultant to start and grow a successful consulting business. Based on her personal experience and research, she discusses financing, defining the right target market, and acquiring and increasing your knowledge base. Throughout the guide, Michelle shares her best practices, and although the guide is specific to building a consulting business around QuickBooks, *many* of the principles apply universally to business in general.

The end that Michelle envisions is the success of individuals willing to invest the energy and passion into creating their own consulting business. This guide is a beginning to achieving this end.

Cheri Streeter, MBA
Director, Small Business Development Center
Overland Park, Kansas

Acknowledgements

I would like to personally acknowledge and express my gratitude to some of those who have contributed to this book:

Cheri Streeter – Her excellent editing skills allowed me to focus on writing. She provided good feedback and kept me focused when I needed it most! She also has given me the opportunity to teach QuickBooks seminars through the Small Business Development Center for many years!

Alison Ball – She provided the encouragement I needed to finish the book. After reading a draft of the book, she provided numerous, beneficial suggestions to help improve the content.

ProAdvisors from across the country – Those who took a few minutes out of their busy day to respond to the survey provided a wealth of information. They shared insightful advice, quotes, and keys to success,

Dawn Scranton and Liz Alexander – Both Dawn and Liz graciously agreed to be interviewed (recorded and transcribed) and featured in the Profiles of Successful QuickBooks Consultants.

All my clients and seminar attendees – They do not realize how much I truly enjoy being able to help them either with QuickBooks or starting and growing their businesses!

Finally, and most importantly, I want to thank my husband, Steve, and my children, Andrew and Jessica, for being so patient and understanding while I worked on my book!

About the Author

Michelle L. Long, CPA is the owner of M. Long Consulting, LLC, which provides QuickBooks consulting and training, business planning and financial consulting to growing businesses and entrepreneurs. She is an Adjunct Professor of Entrepreneurship at Johnson County Community College in Overland Park, Kansas and previously at University of Missouri – Kansas City in Strategic Management and Accounting Systems and Controls courses.

She is an Advanced Certified QuickBooks ProAdvisor, a member of the Certified Trainer Network for Intuit, and a member of the Intuit Speakers Bureau. She facilitates seminars nationally for Intuit's Accountant Training Network. Michelle also conducts a variety of seminars for entrepreneurs and small business owners for both the Missouri and Kansas Small Business Development Centers as well as serves as guest speaker for many non-profit organizations.

Michelle was named a U.S. Small Business Administration's Financial Services Champion of the Year for 2007 in recognition of her dedication to helping entrepreneurs and small business owners.

Michelle is a Certified FastTrac Facilitator and has facilitated the Ewing Marion Kauffman Foundation's FastTrac NewVenture program and Listening to Your Business workshop.

Before starting her own consulting practice, Michelle worked with Price Waterhouse, an international public accounting firm; Baird, Kurtz & Dobson, a regional public accounting firm; and Hallmark Cards, Inc. She earned a Bachelor of Science in Accountancy degree from University of Missouri-Columbia, and an MBA in Entrepreneurship from UMKC.

Table of Contents

Introduction 1
   National Survey of Certified ProAdvisors 5

Chapter 1 - Why Specialize in QuickBooks? 7
   Increasing Number of Potential Clients 7
     New businesses 7
     Existing businesses 8
   Opportunities to Provide Services 9
     Why QuickBooks vs. Other Programs? 9
       Industry Leader 9
       QuickBooks ProAdvisor Program (PAP) 10
       Microsoft's accounting programs 11
       Peachtree by Sage 11
   QuickBooks Consulting with Other Accounting Services 12

Chapter 2 - The Role of the QuickBooks Consultant 15
   Service Opportunities 15
     Software selection 15
     Installation, set-up, and initial training 16
     Training – owner and staff members 18
     Problem solving and trouble shooting 19
     Periodic support or review 20
   Liaison with Accountant or Tax Preparer 21
     Clean up file for year end 21
     Assist with adjusting journal entries 21
     Assist with requests from accountant 22
     When you are the accountant 22
   Consulting – Systems and Procedures 22
     New businesses 22
     Growing businesses 23
   Consulting on Managerial Accounting Issues 23

Custom fields for customers, items, and vendors 24
Reports to help with decision making, marketing, and financial
analysis.. 24
Budgeting and planning 25

Chapter 3 - Are You Ready to Go on Your Own?........................... 27
Personal Characteristics... 27
Education and Expertise 29
Financial Considerations... 31
    Start-up costs... 31
        QuickBooks ProAdvisor Program – $450 31
        Computer – $500 - $2,000 32
        Office Software – $300 - $700.................................... 33
        Office Furniture and Equipment – $100 + ... 33
        Business Cards and Website – $50 - $5,000................. 33
        Other Business Costs – $50 - $2,000 34
    Income considerations 35
Family and Personal Issues.. 36
    Family support 36
    Time commitment and hours 37
Pros and Cons of Being Your Own Boss................................ 38
    Pros 38
    Cons 39
Start-up Stories of Other Consultants 40

Chapter 4 - Improve Your Knowledge Base................................ 41
Use QuickBooks in Your Own Business 41
QuickBooks ProAdvisor Program 42
    Certifications Available 42
    Practice Files.. 43
    Resources 44
Gain Experience... 46
    Work for Another ProAdvisor 46
    Volunteer for Non-Profits 47
    Discount Initially 47

Chapter 5 - Setting up Your Business 49
  Types of Entities 49
  Steps to Getting Started 51
    Federal ID Number 51
    Bank Account and Credit Card 51
    Business Licenses and Permits 52
    Insurance 52
  Set Up Your Office 52
    Business Phone Line 53
    Software Required 53
    Website and E-mail 54
    Equipment, Furniture, and Supplies 55
  Write a Business Plan 56

Chapter 6 - Financial Matters 57
  Create a Budget 57
    Project Income 57
    Expenses 58
    Estimated Taxes 58
  Keep Business and Personal Separate 59
  Manage Cash Flows – Billing and Collecting 59
    Accept Credit Cards 60
  Tax Considerations 60
  Mileage and Other Expenses 61

Chapter 7 - Define Your Services and Billing Rates 63
  Services Provided 63
  Intuit's Annual Billing Rate Survey 65
  Personal Credentials and Expertise 65
  Local Market 67
    Rural vs. City 67
    Competition – Other ProAdvisors 68
  Client Considerations 69
  Services Provided 69
  Hourly vs. Fixed Fee 70

Packaged or Pre-paid Services...70
Pros and Cons – Hourly 71
Pros and Cons – Fixed Fee 71
Other Considerations 72
Discounts—initially and/or non-profits................................72
Billable vs. non-billable time..73

Chapter 8 - Marketing – Initial Considerations 75
Develop Your Identity 75
Name...75
Website 76
Business cards...77
Analyze Competitors 77
Define the Target Market...79

Chapter 9 - Marketing – Methods...81
Find-a-ProAdvisor Website 81
Write Articles...82
Conduct Seminars 83
Referrals...84
Networking...85
Ads in Newsletters 85
Sponsorships 86
Less Effective Methods..86
Trade Shows...87
Traditional Ads 87
National Survey Results...87

Chapter 10 - Performing the Engagement 91
Client Interview 91
Engagement Letters 92
Session Form..94
Newsletters or Communications with Clients..........................94
Invoicing and Collection Procedures 96

Chapter 11 - Growing the Business 99
  Time to Get Help 99
  Control Growth 101
  Moving into an Outside Office 101
  Specialization 102
  Retirement Plans and Benefits 103
  Reevaluate the Structure of Business........................... 104

Chapter 12 - Common Mistakes Consultants Make 107

Chapter 13 - Advice from Other ProAdvisors 111

Chapter 14 - What Consultants Wish They Had Known Sooner...... 123

Chapter 15 - Keys to Success... 131

Appendix A - National ProAdvisor Survey Results 141

Appendix B - Intuit 2007 Rates Survey 149

Appendix C - Profile of Liz Alexander... 155

Appendix D - Profile of Dawn Scranton... 167

Appendix E - Resources.. 178

Introduction

The number of people who dream about starting or owning their own business continues to grow every year. However, there is a big difference between dreaming about it and actually doing it. There are basically four different paths to business ownership:

- ► *Buy an existing business* – You become a business owner right away with this option. You would also acquire existing customers and some name recognition. But, you will need adequate financial resources available to fund the acquisition. You also need to find the right business where the owner is ready to sell.

- ► *Buy a franchise* – When you buy a franchise, it is like getting a "business in a box." You are getting brand recognition in the business name and logo; operating systems, procedures, and manuals; and support and advice to help you succeed. It also requires adequate financial resources (the initial franchise fee can be quite high), a percentage of your income in the future as royalties, and your business decisions are limited to the franchisor's rules.

- ► *Inherit a family business* – This may or may not be an option for you.

- ► *Start from scratch* – This takes more time to get started and there are many details. If it were easy, everyone would do it! But, there are a lot of resources available to help entrepreneurs. You can make all the decisions based on the business you want to build. You also have better control over the financial resources and you can bootstrap to save money.

Many people do not have the financial resources available (or they do not want to risk losing them) to buy an existing business or a franchise. But, what if you could get many of the benefits of a franchise without paying a hefty franchise fee or royalties?

QuickBooks provides national name recognition as the industry leader, training and support, product discounts, and a QuickBooks ProAdvisor Program (PAP) that provides technical support, logos, a referral website, a certification program and even more benefits. Sounds like an easy decision!

If you build a business around QuickBooks, it will provide you with a jumpstart and make owning your own business considerably easier. There are already 3.7 million potential customers currently using QuickBooks and the number keeps growing! According to Intuit's 2006 annual report, there were "approximately 600,000 new QuickBooks customers in 2006— up from approximately 400,000 two years ago."

Plus, there is still a tremendous amount of growth potential in the market. Intuit estimates that there are approximately 15 million more "small- and medium-sized businesses in the United States that do not use any specialized accounting software." QuickBooks is by far the industry leader with somewhere between 85-90% market share of accounting programs for small businesses.

So, as Intuit continues to spend millions on marketing and advertising, research and product development, they are creating new client opportunities for the consultants who support QuickBooks users. Why not grab onto their coat tails and grow your business right along with them?

Because QuickBooks is very flexible and easy to use, once it is set up correctly, users do not usually make a lot of mistakes. However, like any powerful accounting program, it needs to be set up correctly. Many small business owners do not understand accounting or QuickBooks well enough to set it up properly. This is where the QuickBooks consultant is needed to set up the data file and train clients on how to use Quick-Books properly. Sometimes, clients want to learn more about the program to utilize it better and get more information from the system. As a QuickBooks consultant, you can provide the support, training, and assistance that clients need.

So, the bottom line that many people want to know—can you make an adequate or reasonable income from QuickBooks consulting? The simple answer is—yes and no. Yes, there are many QuickBooks consultants who earn over $50,000 and even over $100,000 per year from QuickBooks consulting (in addition to other services provided such as bookkeeping or tax prepara-tion). But, no, you will not earn that much from the very beginning. Like any business, it takes time to grow the business and build your expertise and reputation.

In a National Survey of ProAdvisors (see Appendix A), consultants were asked what their annual gross income was from QuickBooks related consulting and their responses are provided in the following chart.

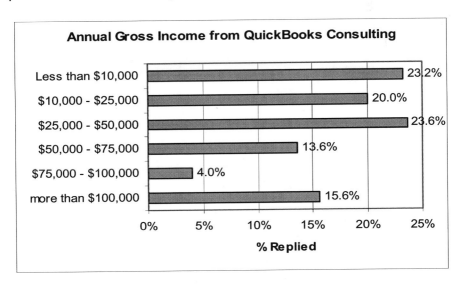

However, you should keep in mind that it takes time to build up your business. Consider the income reported by the consultants along with the number of years that they have been providing QuickBooks consulting services in the following chart.

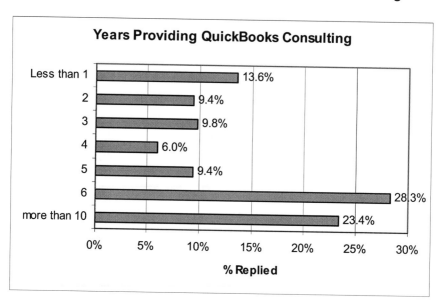

When it comes to start-up costs and financial considerations, there is more good news! You can start a QuickBooks consulting business without a large financial investment, working out of your home, part time while keeping your day job. You probably will not need a loan, have to sign a lease, or have to worry about payroll or overhead costs if you do not want to!

Now, are you ready to get started? This book will help guide you along the way, save you time trying to figure things out, provide useful resources, and help you get started with the keys to success!

National Survey of Certified ProAdvisors

A national survey of Certified ProAdvisors was conducted in August, 2007 and 267 ProAdvisors responded and completed the survey (referred to as "National Survey" throughout the book). Details about the survey, how it was conducted, and all the charts are in Appendix A. The survey was not a scientific survey, and there is no validation of the accuracy of the responses received.

The survey included three open ended questions seeking comments and advice from the consultants:

- ▶ What advice do you have for other/new QuickBooks consultants?

- ▶ What do you wish you would have known sooner or done differently in your business?

- ▶ What would you say are the keys to building a successful QuickBooks consulting business?

There were approximately 300 different comments which are provided in Chapters 13, 14, and 15. In addition, some of the responses are included in text boxes throughout the book (like the one below this paragraph). Many consultants chose to include their name and contact information with their comments and it has been included when available. However, there were also many anonymous comments so you will not see a name with those.

 These text boxes are where you will find some 'keys to success' from the advice, suggestions, and comments provided in the National Survey of ProAdvisors.

Chapter 1

Why Specialize in QuickBooks?

The demand for bookkeeping services, taxes, and other accounting services is well understood and established. The traditional public accounting firm provides most of the traditional accounting services. But, more and more firms (or sole practitioners) are specializing in a niche and creating a boutique firm as a method of differentiation. The niche may be based upon a type of client and specific industries or the focus may be on a specific service provided such as tax planning and preparation.

Can you or your firm specialize in QuickBooks consulting for your niche? Is there sufficient market opportunity in Quick-Books consulting? Can it be a viable revenue stream that is not as seasonal as tax preparation? Does this area offer enough market potential financially? There are several factors to consider before you decide to specialize in QuickBooks consulting—potential clients, types of services possible, support and resources available, as well as income potential.

 "The need for competent QuickBooks consulting is much higher than initially assumed."

Increasing Number of Potential Clients

New businesses

Did you know that there are as many people starting a new business as there are people getting married or having a baby? In 2005, there were approximately 464,000 people starting a new business each *month* according to The Kauffman Index of Entrepreneurial Activity. People of all ages and demographics are starting new businesses in every region of the country. Increasing numbers of baby boomers are starting their own business. This entrepreneurship boom has also spurred many new businesses supporting and helping the other small businesses start and grow—like Quickbooks consulting.

One of the problems entrepreneurs and new business owners face is the recordkeeping required. The Internal Revenue Service requires that each of these new businesses maintains adequate records. If a bank loan or financing are involved, additional reporting and recordkeeping will be required. As a result, there is always a continuous supply of potential new clients that need help setting up and maintaining an accounting system utilizing a program such as QuickBooks.

Existing businesses

In addition to new businesses, in 2006, already about 3.7 million active QuickBooks users existed representing potential clients for QuickBooks consultants. Plus, there is room for continued market penetration into existing businesses. Intuit's 2006 annual report estimates "that approximately 60% of the 26 million small- and medium-sized businesses in the U.S. don't use any specialized accounting software." Thus, ample opportunity exists to obtain clients from existing businesses that finally realize the need for a program such as QuickBooks.

It is amazing the number of existing businesses that still keep their accounting records manually or use Excel spreadsheets and Word invoices. More and more of these businesses are turning to QuickBooks to simplify their recordkeeping and save time. QuickBooks Simple Start allows these types of businesses to start using a computerized accounting program and realize the benefits. Then, as they become more comfortable with computerized accounting, it is easier to upgrade their program to QuickBooks Pro or Premier.

Opportunities to Provide Services

A QuickBooks consultant can support these millions of small businesses starting with the initial set up of QuickBooks. The consultant may provide training to the owner and/or employees on the proper way to enter transactions. In addition, there is a wealth of opportunities for trouble-shooting and fixing mistakes and problems clients have with their data files. The consultant can also offer suggestions to track additional information (creating types of customers, tracking additional custom fields, and more) that will provide the owner and management with additional information for marketing, strategic planning, and more.

Additionally, growing businesses often outgrow their initial accounting system. This provides the consultant with the opportunity to help clients determine their needs, redefine processes and procedures, and implement a new accounting system. Intuit has created the family of programs to grow with the business. It is possible to start with QuickBooks Simple Start, move up to QuickBooks Pro and/or Premier, and ultimately to QuickBooks Enterprise. This allows the consultant the opportunity to continue providing services to clients for many years.

Why QuickBooks vs. Other Programs?

Industry Leader

QuickBooks is the undisputed industry leader with 85-90% market share. As a consultant, why not associate yourself with the industry leader that provides significantly more potential clients than the others. Do you really have the time and inclination to maintain an expert knowledge base in more than one program, or would it be better to focus on the most widely used program—QuickBooks?

In addition, potential customers will often ask other business owners, friends, or associates what accounting program they use, which is usually some version of QuickBooks. It is easier for customers to get the support and help they need if they choose QuickBooks as opposed to another program. They can get help from a number of sources including the many other QuickBooks users; QuickBooks (Intuit's) support options, or a QuickBooks ProAdvisor.

"Don't be a consultant on all software out there, dedicate to it so you can really provide quality services. If you are in over your head, admit it and get help."

QuickBooks ProAdvisor Program (PAP)

The QuickBooks ProAdvisor Program is for CPAs, accountants, bookkeepers and consultants at a modest fee (currently $449 per year as of this printing) to help us in a variety of ways. Your annual membership fee includes QuickBooks Premier Accountant edition, a one-user edition of QuickBooks Enterprise, as well as the following benefits:

► Technical Support – a dedicated phone number that is available 24/7 so you always have a partner to consult with on technical questions.

► Certification – a way to differentiate yourself and improve your knowledge base. This is covered in greater detail in Chapter 4 on Improving Your Knowledge Base.

► Find-a-ProAdvisor Website – a great way to get new clients at no additional cost!

► Resources – articles, webinars, and more to help you market and grow your practice, train your clients, and more.

► Community Boards – another great way to get support and help and you can learn a lot by reading the questions and answers from others.

► Software – in addition to the programs mentioned above, you can get Simple Start or trial versions free to give to clients (or potential clients).

There are more details on the QuickBooks ProAdvisor Program (PAP) and the benefits at the website: account-ant.intuit.com. If you want to be a QuickBooks consultant, you really should join the program—you need the software every year anyway which is included with your annual membership fee.

Microsoft's Accounting Programs

Microsoft has made several attempts over the years to gain market share in the area of small business accounting programs, but they have been unable to truly challenge Quick-Books' leadership position. Their most recent attempt is Microsoft Office Accounting Professional 2007 (Accounting 2007) and a more limited version called Accounting Express 2007 (which they offer for free).

Microsoft is trying to emphasize that Accounting 2007 in-tegrates with Word, Excel, and Outlook. However, QuickBooks also integrates with these programs. Accounting 2007 has a similar look and feel to the older versions of QuickBooks (2005 and prior). However, it appears that these programs still lack the depth and sophistication of QuickBooks.

Peachtree by Sage

Peachtree was once a widely used accounting program and the favorite of accountants. However, QuickBooks pro-duced a more user-friendly program with icons and flowcharts that is more appealing to users without an accounting back-ground. Over the years, QuickBooks added more and more features to its program and listened to the recommendations from accountants. As QuickBooks gained market share, Peachtree lost market share.

Many accountants still like Peachtree and are comfortable using it; and many colleges and universities still use it in their accounting programs. However, the reality is that not that many businesses still use Peachtree and the number continues to decline. Thus, the number of potential clients is significantly smaller and declining—not a great market opportunity!

Numerous businesses have already converted from Peachtree to QuickBooks. As businesses upgrade their computer and accounting system, they are switching to QuickBooks. When looking for help, they find that there are very few certified consultants for Peachtree (search the Peachtree website for a consultant in your city and compare the difference to a search for a QuickBooks ProAdvisor). In fact, the number of Peachtree consultants *worldwide* (500) is less than one-half of one percent when compared to the number of QuickBooks ProAdvisors (over 40,000).

QuickBooks Consulting with Other Accounting Services

QuickBooks consulting is a natural extension of services for a traditional accounting practice. Many QuickBooks consultants also provide tax preparation and bookkeeping services. In contrast to tax preparation, QuickBooks consulting is not as seasonal and can provide income year round. The following chart shows the other services consultants provide based on their responses in the National Survey of ProAdvisors.

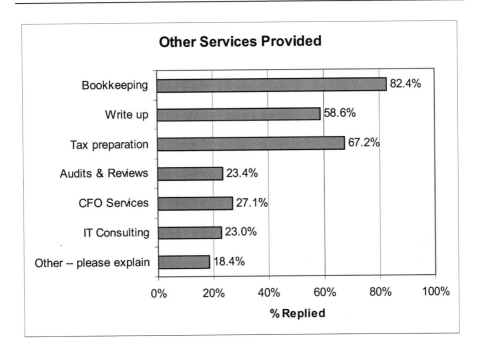

Other Services Provided

Bookkeeping	82.4%
Write up	58.6%
Tax preparation	67.2%
Audits & Reviews	23.4%
CFO Services	27.1%
IT Consulting	23.0%
Other -- please explain	18.4%

% Replied

Some accountants are reluctant to support clients doing their own bookkeeping, thinking they would lose the income from providing those services. However, that is a short-term viewpoint. If clients are trained to use QuickBooks, they still will need accounting advice for taxes, depreciation, buying and selling assets, and a number of other issues that arise. In addition, as their business grows or employees are added, they may need assistance training new bookkeepers, learning pay-roll, upgrading to another version of QuickBooks, or more financial and managerial consulting. You can also assist clients with sales tax returns, internal controls consulting, third-party software integration, and quarterly check ups. So you will probably not lose clients, but instead will change the type of services that are being provided.

As clients gain knowledge and understanding of their own accounting, there also may be more opportunity to provide other financial advice and management consulting services to those clients. The consulting services most likely will have a higher billing rate than the bookkeeping services and can replace the lost income from the bookkeeping services previously provided for clients. In addition, you may find that you become a more trusted advisor to clients rather than merely providing them with bookkeeping services. This in turn can lead to more referrals from clients since you are looking out for their best interests and not merely your own fees.

Chapter 2

The Role of the QuickBooks Consultant

If you have decided to specialize in QuickBooks consulting, either on your own or within your existing accounting practice, you may wonder what role a QuickBooks consultant actually plays. Where does the consultant fit in if there is an accountant or auditor, tax preparer, and maybe an outside payroll service? It will be helpful to take a look at the role of the QuickBooks consultant with the basic service opportunities as a liaison with the accountant or tax preparer, as a consultant about the accounting system and procedures, and by providing managerial accounting recommendations.

Service Opportunities

Software selection

Some clients are not sure which version of the Quick-Books family they should get—Simple Start, Pro, Premier, Online, or Enterprise. They will ask for your recommendation for their business. This is why it is important for consultants to understand the different features available and the number of user licenses available in each version of QuickBooks. The consultant should interview clients to identify their specific needs now as well as potential needs within the next three years. For example, clients may plan to add payroll capabilities within a year or to increase the number of user licenses. The software selected should allow for some growth before they have to upgrade.

If clients have special industry related needs that Quick-Books does not meet, there are hundreds of third-party, add-on programs that have been written to integrate with QuickBooks. The consultant may need to explore and research some of these for clients. The best place to start is at the website <u>marketplace.intuit.com</u>.

Some consultants even specialize in third-party applications and integration such as Dawn Scranton, owner of Accounting Directors, Inc. in West Palm Beach, Florida. Dawn is the author of <u>Quickbooks Add-on's and Integration Consulting</u> and formed the Association of QuickBooks Technologists to support consultants in this specialized area. (See Appendix D for an interview with Dawn).

Installation, set-up, and initial training

Every month there are a large number of new businesses, in addition to existing businesses, that are ready to begin using QuickBooks. Sometimes, clients will buy and install the software themselves. Then, as they begin trying to set it up and use it, they often realize that they need some help. QuickBooks is very easy to use once it is set up properly. However, if it is not set up correctly, the garbage in, garbage out theory applies. This is why it is best if clients get help with the initial set up and training. Then, they will start using the program properly from the beginning.

It is preferable to have clients purchase and install QuickBooks themselves before you begin to work with them. It helps demonstrate their commitment to using the program and gets them actively involved from the beginning.

However, you could have clients that want you to install QuickBooks and set up the computer hardware as well so you need to be prepared. Particularly if it is a retail client, then you need to be sure you know how to set up and configure the point of sale hardware (cash register, receipt printer, scanner, and credit card reader). Be aware that QuickBooks Point of Sale is tricky to set up if you do not have experience with it. Initially, it is advisable to work with a ProAdvisor who has experience working with point of sale clients and preferable is a Certified QuickBooks Point of Sale ProAdvisor.

Regarding initial file set-up, many consultants have a standard company file for each of the various industries they work with frequently. For example, the consultant may have a standard file for service businesses, contractors, and retail clients. The standard file usually includes a customized chart of accounts, customized preferences, and may include some initial items. They start with this standard file instead of going through the interview or initial set-up every time and then you can customize the file for the particular client. It is important to interview clients about their business and how they operate so that you can properly configure and customize QuickBooks for their business.

 "Standardize instead of customize!"

Special care needs to be taken when entering beginning balances and open transactions as of the start date. You do not want to get your client started off on the wrong foot! If you need help or additional information on setting up beginning balances, there are resources available to help you learn. Consult the ProAdvisor website, The Sleeter Group's <u>Consultant's Reference Guide</u> or other books may provide guidance as well.

Next, the consultant should train clients on how to enter transactions for their business. It is helpful to have clients enter a couple of each type of different transactions (checks, invoices, etc.) while you are there to ensure that they are doing it properly. Make sure they understand the chart of accounts and items list and how they are related and function.

Training – owner and staff members

A QuickBooks consultant needs to be able to train others on how to properly enter transactions and use the program. It is important to be able to relate to clients or QuickBooks users at their level of understanding. Some clients will already be familiar with accounting or bookkeeping and may have used other programs in the past. On the other hand, some clients do not even balance their own checkbooks manually!

It is important that the consultant have patience and understanding and NEVER make clients feel stupid, slow, or inadequate. If you try explaining it and they do not understand it, then you should try to explain it another way that may make more sense to them. Individuals have different learning styles with some people being more verbal, some more visual, and others have to do it (hands-on) several times and think it over to understand the concept.

Sometimes the business owner has someone else doing the bookkeeping, but the owner realizes a need to also understand their QuickBooks program. This is important and should be encouraged in the event the bookkeeper is sick or otherwise unavailable. However, the owner may only want to be able to generate and customize reports to help with managing the business. So, the consultant should discuss with clients how much detail they want to understand about QuickBooks. Do they want to be able to enter transactions or merely be able to review the financial information and generate reports?

Another training opportunity arises whenever there are new employees or changes in job duties. If the bookkeeper quits, there may be an especially urgent need for training someone to take over the duties.

A company may wish to have a private training session for a couple of employees who are already using the program. They may be interested in cross training the employees to do other duties, or they may want to learn to utilize the program capabilities more fully.

Some consultants also provide training seminars either on their own or in connection with a local Small Business Development Center (SBDC) or other organization. This is a great method of developing a market for training larger groups of users and a good marketing tool—which is covered more in Chapter 9 on Marketing Methods.

Problem solving and trouble shooting

Problem solving and trouble shooting are big opportunities for QuickBooks consultants! Often, clients will set up the program themselves and start entering transactions. At some point (a few months, six months, or a year or more), they realize that something is wrong. The numbers do not look right and they are not quite sure what is wrong. Or, they may realize what they did wrong, but they do not know how to fix it. Sometimes they are afraid to fix it, because they do not want to make it worse.

This is a difficult area that you will get better at fixing with more experience. Sometimes it is hard to know whether you should start fresh with a new file and re-enter the data instead of trying to fix it. There are several factors to consider including: how many transactions have been entered, what exactly needs fixing, and do they have the time and are they willing to start over? Every situation seems to be unique in some way. The consultant needs to evaluate each case and weigh the time and cost of fixing their current file with the time and cost of starting over. It is best to present both scenarios to clients and guide them to make the ultimate decision.

> *KEY TO SUCCESS—"Experience, honesty and perhaps most importantly creative thinking, as every client is different even when there are many similarities."*
> *Paulette Dreher, SBS Associates, Inc., Westwood, NJ*

Initially, you may need to do some research to learn how to fix specific problems. There are several resources available: QuickBooks community bulletin boards are helpful, as well as the <u>Consultant's Reference Guide</u> by The Sleeter Group. If you are a ProAdvisor, you will have access to a dedicated technical support hotline number that is available 24/7 to help you.

Periodic support or review

After clients have been using QuickBooks for awhile and they get more comfortable with it, they will not require as much support. However, they may have occasional questions or transactions that they are not sure how to enter.

> *"Try to solve your clients' pain points rather than just teach them how to use QuickBooks. Make yourself their go-to person when they have questions, they call you."*
> *Dawn Ashpole, SBA Services, Inc., Portland, OR*

Some consultants offer packages of time to be used over a period of time. For example, clients may purchase a three-hour support package which they can use as they have questions or need help. This works well for the quick phone consultations or remote access when clients do not have too many questions. You can offer the three-hour package at a minor discount off your normal billing rates or you can use your standard billing rates; but give clients a guarantee that you will respond to the question within a certain amount of time.

Quarterly reviews or 'tune-ups' are other services that many consultants offer. This is a good practice to make corrections all year long as opposed to waiting until year end to clean up the data files. This also provides the opportunity to train clients better in the areas of the mistakes. You want to ensure clients are getting accurate data to manage their business.

The amount of support required will vary based upon the clients' abilities and the complexity of their business. You should try to meet the needs of all clients while seeking referrals for new clients.

Liaison with Accountant or Tax Preparer

Clients who already have an outside accountant, auditor, or tax preparer can still benefit from the use of a QuickBooks consultant. Sometimes the consultant can provide some additional accounting help to clients around year end.

Clean up file for year end

The consultant can help clients 'clean up' and correct mistakes or mispostings prior to turning the file over to the accountant or tax preparer. For example, clients may need to write off some accounts receivable or to accrue expenses. These are more difficult transactions that may require help from the QuickBooks consultant.

Assist with adjusting journal entries

Often, the accountant or tax preparer gives clients some adjusting journal entries to enter. Sometimes clients just do not want to enter a journal entry—the whole debit and credit thing scares them! Other times, the account names used in the journal entries do not exactly match the names in the clients' chart of accounts so they do not know which account to use. It is important that clients enter the adjusting journal entries and the consultant can help ensure clients get it done correctly. Then, the consultant should also create a closing date password as of year end so clients do not inadvertently make changes to the prior year—a common occurrence!

Also, clients using an outside payroll service usually need help with how to enter the payroll into QuickBooks. There are different methods to record payroll and the consultant should choose the method the client would be most comfortable using. Then, using the payroll reports train clients how to enter the amounts to properly record payroll.

Assist with requests from accountant

Accountants may request certain reports or information from clients who are not sure exactly what is being requested. The consultant can help translate the request from the accountant or tax preparer and get the information requested. This may require modifying or customizing a report which the consultant can do for clients.

When you are the accountant

QuickBooks Premier Accountant edition will allow you to work with client files and allow you to do their payroll, depreciation, and tax returns as well. Accountants will really appreciate the Fixed Asset Manager, Working Trial Balance, reversing journal entries and more include in QuickBooks Premier Accoutant Edition. In addition, QuickBooks integrates beautifully with Lacerte and ProSeries tax software simplifying your workflow at year end!

Consulting – Systems and Procedures

New businesses

When setting up a QuickBooks file and asking clients how their business operates, the consultant may discover that they have not yet established any systems or procedures. The consultant should help clients establish procedures for how orders are taken, money is collected and deposited, expenses are incurred and paid.

Even if it is just the owner, the consultant should discuss good internal control procedures in preparation for future employees. Clients may need help with what documents to keep and how to file them. They may also need to be informed about sales and use taxes and payroll taxes. If clients use subcontractors, then the consultant should also tell them about 1099s and the related requirements.

Growing businesses

As the business grows and adds employees, the consultant needs to be proactive advising the owner about good internal control practices. Duties should be segregated as much as possible and employees should be cross trained and rotate duties periodically.

At some point, clients may find that the version of QuickBooks they are using no longer meets their needs. That is where Intuit has done a great job of offering products for small businesses to grow into. Clients can move from Simple Start, to Pro or Premier, and up to Enterprise edition which supports up to twenty users.

Consulting on Managerial Accounting Issues

In addition to the financial accounting provided by QuickBooks, the consultant can help clients set up the program to track information for managerial purposes and decision making.

"Learn managerial accounting - too many CPAs only care about tax accounting. So it is easy to differentiate from their services."

Custom fields for customers, items, and vendors

This is an area where the consultant can provide suggestions that clients may have never even known are available. What additional information could they track about customers, vendors, employees, and items? For example, clients could keep track of customer birthdates to send out a card with a coupon enclosed. There are many different ways to use the custom fields, and they can help with marketing, customer relations, and managerial reports for managing the business.

Reports to help with decision making, marketing, and financial analysis

Many clients never really explore all the reports that are available to them. They usually find the basic financial reports, but they miss many of other reports that could help them in the management of their business. For example, the sales by item report can help a retailer allocate shelf space to the best selling items.

When you are talking with clients about how their business operates, you should be considering which reports might be helpful to clients in the management of their business. Clients should also be shown how to look for trends and changes from one period to the next to help identify potential problems areas.

Another service you can offer your clients is to create custom financial statements for them including footnotes and management letters. Using QuickBooks Premier Accountant Edition's Financial Statement Designer, you can customize these reports for clients once and then generate them quickly either monthly or quarterly. This helps cement your relationship with them and keeps them coming back because they cannot create these reports themselves (unless they are using Quick-Books Enterprise.

Budgeting and planning

It is surprising how many clients do not realize that they can enter budget numbers into QuickBooks. This allows them to get monthly reports comparing budget to actual. This is especially helpful when cash flow is tight and maintaining a budget is crucial. If they are going to need additional funding, they need to be aware of it sooner rather than later.

The consultant can also help clients with preparing a budget. This is an area that is difficult for many business own-ers, but it can help them be more successful. By creating a budget and tracking how the actual performance compares to the budget, it can help clients say no to certain expenditures if they are not in the budget.

KEY TO SUCCESS—"Know your Accounting better than you know QuickBooks. Be flexible with applying your QuickBooks and accounting knowledge with clients. Talk about their business and how they like to do things, if they need the detail of job costing or are fine with just showing income and expense. Try to put yourself in their place and keep it as simple as possible. Introduce more complex methods to those that can handle it, but always step back when you feel they are getting overwhelmed. There is no such thing as the "correct" way to use QuickBooks, customize the process to what works for them, or they won't want to use QuickBooks."

Karen Cook, Wayne A Blosberg, PA, Coon Rapids, MN.

Chapter 3

Are You Ready to Go on Your Own?

It is both exciting and scary to think about going on your own and starting your own consulting business. Based on the material in this chapter, you may realize that you are definitely ready to go on your own and are anxious to get started. However, you may realize that you are not really ready at this time and decide to wait. It is better to wait until you are ready, because starting and growing your own business takes a lot of time, energy, and dedication.

Personal Characteristics

There are certain characteristics that are needed to be a successful QuickBooks consultant. Some of these may come naturally to you, while others may need some work to develop them.

- Motivation and determination – It is not easy to start your own business, and it takes a lot of motivation and determination to see it through. If you do not have that inner drive, it may be tough making it through some of the more difficult times.

- Communication – You will need to communicate effectively with lots of people both written and orally. Whether it is on your website, via email or phone, in networking meetings or luncheons, you need to be able to convey your message in a clear and convincing manner.

► Listening Skills – It is very important to listen to the needs and problems of clients. You should ask pertinent questions so that you are able to fully understand the issues and problems. It is critical to properly define the problems and issues so that you can recommend the appropriate solution. You need to let the client do most of the talking while you listen.

"The keys to building a successful QuickBooks consulting business are specifically to 'listen' to what the client wants to accomplish and make recommendations in order for the client to accomplish these goals."

► Interpersonal skills – Building and growing a consulting business requires developing relationships and cultivating referrals. You also need to be able to deal effectively with problem clients.

"You must love people, Quickbooks, and business. A QuickBooks consultant needs to be proficient in all three."

► Flexibility – Nothing ever goes exactly as planned, and unexpected events are common occurrences. You need to be able to adapt to the current situation and be willing to make changes as they are needed.

► Persistence – You cannot expect clients to start calling and to get referrals simply because you are in business. It takes time, planning, and action to build and grow your own business. You have to be persistent in your marketing and networking efforts and realize that it will take time to see the results in the form of referrals.

▶ Self-confidence – If you do not have confidence in your-self and your abilities, then clients will not have confidence in you either. You may be unsure of yourself at times, but you have to hide your uncertainties. If you present yourself as capable and confident, then others will perceive you as such.

"Don't underestimate your abilities, and don't under price your services. Consider travel time to and from clients, and consider research time and price accordingly. Remember, YOU are the EXPERT!"

Education and Expertise

There are no rules or regulations related specifically to QuickBooks consulting, so theoretically anyone could say he/she is a QuickBooks consultant. However, if you do not have a certain amount of education and expertise, you probably will not be very successful for very long. Here we will look at some of the minimum qualifications that you should possess, and in the next chapter, we will explore how to build your exper-tise and further your knowledge base.

▶ Bookkeeping or accounting education – at a minimum, you should have a solid understanding of basic book-keeping. You need to understand basic accounting concepts, such as journal entries (including debits and credits), charts of accounts, financial reports, etc. Clients will make mistakes and as the consultant, you need the knowledge to make corrections. Without a solid book-keeping or accounting background, you should not begin consulting yet. You should consider taking accounting classes at the local community college (for credit or non credit) if you need to learn more.

"A successful QuickBooks consultant must have a strong accounting background in order to apply the QuickBooks processes that are best suited to a particular client and industry. QuickBooks consulting is far more than training someone on the functions of QuickBooks - the Help file and books can do that. You have to train a client how to use QuickBooks in a manner that leads to producing accurate financial information and introduce them to the capabilities of financial decision-making based on the reliable financial data from QuickBooks. Once you learn to provide a well-rounded service to your clients, the referrals will come."
Karen Cook, Wayne A Blosberg, PA, Coon Rapids, MN.

▶ Business experience – You should have some business experience (at least three to five years). As a QuickBooks consultant, you will need to understand in general how clients' businesses operate, as well as how other businesses operate so that you can make suggestions or improvements. Understanding business operations is best learned from experience, and if you can work in several different types of businesses, that is even better.

▶ Computer knowledge – You don't have to be a computer "techie" but you will need a certain level of computer knowledge to be successful. You should understand the basics of computer security and processes (firewalls, anti-virus, back-ups, and remote access). Again, consider taking classes or seminars if you need to learn more in this area.

▶ QuickBooks knowledge – You should have a very good understanding of the program and have used it yourself extensively. We will discuss how to build your expertise in the next chapter, but initially you should have some knowledge and familiarity with the program.

"Never never call yourself a QuickBooks Consultant UNLESS you know the software inside out. Learning the QuickBooks software thoroughly is your very first step."

▶ Degrees and certifications – If you have an accounting degree or certification (CPA, CMA, etc.), then you are better prepared to specialize in QuickBooks consulting. You should be able to charge somewhat higher fees based on your credentials, but you still need to make sure that you have the expertise in QuickBooks. Again, we will discuss how to build your expertise in the next chapter.

KEY TO SUCCESS—"Without a doubt, a combination of educa-tion and experience--you HAVE to know the accounting for the decisions you make as you record and you have to know the accounting of what QuickBooks is doing (that you might not see). The experience in both industry and with QuickBooks makes you worthy of charging a fee for your services. The accounting experience helps you guide your clients and customize client reports-- and the QuickBooks experience helps you set up & problem solve within the software in a professionally effective manner. There is always more to learn."
Debbi C. Warden, CPA, MBA, The Business Manager, LLC
Centennial, CO 80122

Financial Considerations

Start-up costs

The great thing about starting a QuickBooks consulting business is that you can minimize your start-up costs. It is possible to start on your own working out of your home and even part time.

QuickBooks ProAdvisor Program – $450

You will need QuickBooks Premier Accountant Edition (MSRP $449 as of this printing) version of the program so that you can support clients regardless of the version of the program they are using (Pro, Premier Contractor, Premier Manufacturing, etc.). Plus, you should probably have several years (and versions if you do not have QuickBooks Premier Accountant Edition) of QuickBooks installed on your computer for clients who have not upgraded to the current year (if you are working with clients' data files and sending it back to them, you need to work with the file in the same year of the program that they use). If you are just starting and you need older versions of QuickBooks, you can usually buy them on eBay. Some consultants only support the past three years of the software, while other consultants will support the past five years. Generally, clients should upgrade their software at least every three years. After three years, Intuit no longer supports the software and it is harder to get checks or forms printed for the older versions as well.

Instead of just buying the software, you should join QuickBooks ProAdvisor Program (PAP) for $449 (as of this printing). You will get QuickBooks Premier Accountant Edition software plus the many other benefits mentioned earlier. Again, check out accountant.intuit.com for all the benefits and details of the program.

Computer – $500 - $2,000

If you don't have a newer computer (three years old or less), then you will need to purchase one. You might consider buying a notebook instead of a desktop. You can take the notebook to clients, to conduct seminars, or when traveling. Computer prices have continued to decline and you can get a desktop or notebook for as low as $500 if you shop around. It is not necessary to buy the top of the line computer—QuickBooks is not like a game that requires very large amounts of graphics or memory.

You should also have a good backup solution since your business is so dependent on your computer data. You might consider using an online backup service for its convenience and reliability. QuickBooks has an online backup service for as little as $4.95-$14.95/month (as of this printing) with discounts for annual subscriptions and you can back up data other than just your QuickBooks files. It is a small price to pay for insurance to protect your critical data.

Office Software – $300 - $700

If you do not already have them, you will need some basic software programs including: Internet security, anti-virus, and probably Microsoft Office. You will need Microsoft Word for many tasks and Microsoft Excel to import or export data in QuickBooks or work with client spreadsheets. Many consultants use Microsoft Outlook to manage their email and calendar. If you will be conducting or presenting seminars, you will also want Microsoft PowerPoint. If you want to design business cards, letterhead, flyers, websites or other promotional pieces, you may want Microsoft Publisher.

Office Furniture and Equipment – $100 +

Although much of your work may be performed at the client's office, you will probably want to set up your own office or place to work. At a minimum you'll need at least a desk and chair, a file cabinet and bookshelves. You may need some office equipment including: an office phone and answering machine, shredder, printer or copier/scanner/fax machine. Many cities have places where you can buy used office furniture and/or equipment and it can be in very good condition at a great price!

Business Cards and Website – $50 - $5,000

You need professional business cards—do not try to print your own! There are many online printing companies that can produce nice cards relatively inexpensively. The quality of the business cards from www.overnightprints.com is very impressive, affordable, and delivered fast. You can get 1,000 business cards (full color) for around $50 (or 100 for $10) and they are on heavy cardstock! Another company to consider is www.vistaprints.com, and there are other companies as well if you search on the Internet.

As for a website, there are different viewpoints. It is my opinion that you must have a website to be considered professional and credible. When you meet potential clients or they find your name on the Find-a-ProAdvisor website, they will want to go to your website to learn more about you. Your website is your brochure; providing information about the services you provide, testimonials from clients, information about you and how to contact you.

You do not have to have a professionally designed website, but it should not appear cheap either. You can pay $500 to $5,000 to have your website designed for you. Or, there is software available (including Microsoft Publisher) to use to design your own website. As a ProAdvisor, you can get a free, professionally-designed 3 page website for one year from Homestead. You will also receive discounts for additional pages or to continue after the first 12 months. You can find the details at www.qbadvisor.com under the Practice resources, Grow Your Practice section.

Keep in mind that your website is a reflection of your business image and should be consistent with your business cards and letterhead. We will talk more about your website and email in Chapter 5 on Setting up Your Business and Chapter 8 on Marketing.

Other Business Costs – $50 - $2,000

You probably will need a business license or permit for your city, state or county. You may need to file a Registration of a Fictitious Name if you are a sole-proprietor and using a name other than your own name. If you decide to set your business up as a Limited Liability Company (LLC), Partnership, or Corporation, there will be fees associated with setting up those entities as well. You can learn about these fees on the secretary of state's website for the state where your business is located. If you have a lawyer do this for you, you can expect attorney's fees to be around $500 to $2,000 depending upon the complexity of the business structure you choose to set up. You can also use Intuit's MyCorporation (www.MyCorp.com) to file the documents to form an LLC or corporation for as little as $149 (as of this printing) plus state filing fees and shipping. Entity types and considerations are discussed more in Chapter 5 on Setting up Your Business.

Income considerations

Your financial situation will be different depending on your age, marital status, family size, geographic location, and lifestyle. You should assess your current financial situation and determine your monthly income requirements. There are several things to think about including:

- ▶ Are you going to start your business part time or full time?

- ▶ Will you have another source of income?

- ▶ What are your personal minimum monthly expenses and how can you reduce them? Can you cut back from the premium cable package to a basic package? Can you skip Starbucks every day? You may need to look for ways to reduce your discretionary monthly expenses during the start-up years of your business.

- ▶ Do you have adequate savings to help cover monthly expenses? You should realize that it will take several years to build up the income potential of your business. It usually takes time (three to five years) to build and grow a consulting business.

▶ If you start with a home office, you can really minimize your monthly business expenses. A consulting business can provide great profit margins and cash flow, but remember it will take time to build the business.

▶ What income levels are possible from a QuickBooks consulting business? As previously mentioned in the introduction, it is possible to earn over $100,000 a year providing QuickBooks related consulting services. In fact, one third of the ProAdvisors in the National Survey earned over $50,000 a year.

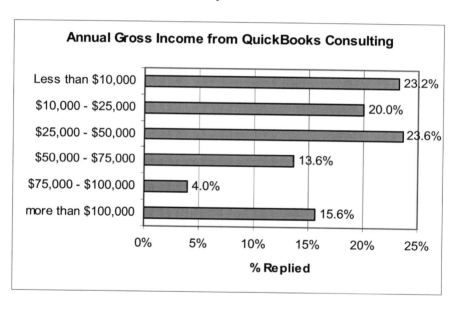

Family and Personal Issues

Family support

If you have a family or significant other, you should include them in your business planning and considerations. It takes a lot of time and energy to start your own business and you will need the support and understanding of your family. If they do not support you, then it makes it much harder to be successful at both work and family life. You need to communicate with your family about your plans and listen to their comments and concerns.

You also need to consider your family life when determining what hours you will work. It is feasible to be available to clients 24/7 and on vacations, but is that good for your family life? It is okay to tell clients that you will be on vacation or having some family time and that they should only contact you in an emergency. Be sure to communicate your office hours when you initially sign up the client and always give plenty of notice when you will be unavailable for an extended time. Most clients will actually respect you for setting those limits.

However, there may be times when clients are in a difficult situation and they really do need your help and support when you are on vacation. What if their bookkeeper quits unexpectedly and they cannot pay bills, invoice customers, or create payroll? As your own boss, you can decide if and when you want to make arrangements to be available on weekends or vacations. Discuss the situation with your family so that they understand the circumstances when you make arrangements like that with a client.

Time commitment and hours

As you get busier, it is easy for the work hours to expand and get out of control. You should consider whether or not you want to work nights or weekends. Sometimes, clients want to meet outside of normal work hours for a variety of reasons. It is great for customer service if you can be accommodating. You may want to make appointments only one night a week and/or certain times on the weekends. However, if you have younger kids with soccer games or specified bedtimes, you may not want to do that very much at this point in time. As the kids get older, then you may reconsider your policies. It is a personal decision, but one that you should think about so you know how to respond to client requests.

The nice thing about being your own boss is that you can schedule when you will work and meet with clients. If your child has a field trip that you want to go on, you can block it off on your schedule. You can schedule client appointments around doctor, dentist, or other personal appointment. You can volunteer for the Parent Teacher Association (PTA) or other school activities if you choose (also good networking for your business).

Pros and Cons of Being Your Own Boss

Pros

Many people dream about being their own boss! For some people, that is a primary motivator for starting their own business. As the boss, you get to make almost all of the rules—until clients prompt you to change your rules! Basically you have control and you can decide:

▶ What hours and days you want to work—you control your own schedule as described above.

▶ What types of clients and engagements you will accept—you can decide whether or not you accept a client. There are some clients you may want to refer to others for a variety of reasons. Liz Alexander (owner of Elizabeth Alexander, CPA, Arlington, Texas) prefers not to work in the manufacturing industry, so she refers them to other ProAdvisors. She discusses this and more in an interview which you can read in Appendix C or listen to at www.mlongconsulting.com.

▶ Specialties you want to concentrate on—if you are interested in a certain industry, type of client, or other area,
you can choose to pursue that specialty. (Specialties are
discussed in more depth in Chapter 7 – Define Your Services and Billing Rates and in Chapter 11 – Growing the
Business).

Cons

Being your own boss is not always that wonderful. There
are many drawbacks and unforeseen events that occur. Some
things you may discover include:

▶ You will generally work longer and harder than you anticipated. Ask any small business owner or entrepreneur
and they will tell you that they work much harder for
themselves than they ever did as an employee! If you do
not work, you do not get paid!

 *"Let everyone know you are in business and work 60 hours a
week." Keith Gormezano, A Better Temporary, Inc., Seattle, WA*

▶ Initially, you probably will be responsible for everything!
Most likely you will not have an Information Technology
(IT) department to call when your computer crashes. If
you run out of office supplies, it is your own fault! You
have to do the invoicing, collecting, paying bills, and all
other administrative tasks.

▶ Instead of having one boss, you now have many
bosses—all your clients become your boss. You are
working to please them and keep them happy. It is not
always easy!

► You are responsible for the marketing of your business. If you are not marketing, you will not get new clients. It is an ongoing task that you should allocate time for every week.

► When something unexpected occurs you have to handle it and deal with it! It does not matter whose fault it was— you have to solve the problem.

Start-up Stories of Other Consultants

You can read what Dawn Scranton and Liz Alexander had to say about their start up experiences in their interviews in Appendix C and D. You can also listen to the interviews or download them from www.mlongconsulting.com.

Chapter 4

Improve Your Knowledge Base

Before you start your own QuickBooks consulting business, you may need to improve your knowledge base. It is critical that you know the product very well! You do not have to be an expert to get started, but you should not accept any client engagements that you are not qualified for.

"I probably would have attended more training sessions before I hung my shingle."

"Be willing to say NO to potential clients who don't fit my areas of interest or expertise. Make contact with other Advisors, so I can refer them to someone more appropriate."

Use QuickBooks in Your Own Business

As you start your new business, you should set up your own company in QuickBooks. You need to use the program as much as possible. It is also a good idea to try to utilize all the various features QuickBooks has to offer in your own business. Using the program for your own business helps clients realize that you "practice what you preach."

"Use QuickBooks yourself. Setup A/P, A/R, play with different invoices, loading Logo's, etc. Learn how to setup payroll and sales tax items, as these will be one of the first questions a new client will ask you." Scott Fullerton CPA, Blue Springs, MO

QuickBooks ProAdvisor Program

Joining the QuickBooks ProAdvisor Program (PAP) could be considered the first step to building a successful QuickBooks consulting business. At a relatively modest cost ($449 as of this printing), you get software, technical support, and a wealth of resources and support to help you succeed in your consulting business. You should research all that the program has to offer at: accountant.intuit.com.

Certifications Available

If you want to build a successful QuickBooks consulting business, you should start by obtaining some (or all) of the certifications available. By earning the certifications, you increase and strengthen your knowledge of QuickBooks products. Being certified also helps build credibility with clients. Intuit offers several different certifications for ProAdvisors:

► Certified QuickBooks ProAdvisor

► Advanced Certified QuickBooks ProAdvisor

► Certified QuickBooks Point of Sale ProAdvisor

► Certified QuickBooks Enterprise ProAdvisor

Intuit provides lessons (webinars and handouts) that you can download from the Internet and view as your schedule allows. The lessons cover various QuickBooks topics and prepare you for the certification exams. Each certification has different requirements to achieve it. Generally, you have to pass an examination (three parts for the basic certification) with a score of 85% or higher.

The examinations are not real easy and you may find yourself reviewing the webinars (lessons) again to help you pass the test (you get 99 tries to get a score of at least 85%).

The webinars and examinations help you improve your knowledge base about QuickBooks products and features. Even if you are an experienced QuickBooks user, you can always learn something new (or remember something forgotten).

After you pass the initial certification and become a Certified QuickBooks ProAdvisor, there are several benefits available to you! Some of these (logos, Find-a-ProAdvisor website) are discussed in more detail in Chapter 9 on Marketing Methods.

Practice Files

Practice files (or sample company files) are a great way to improve your knowledge base. Practice files are available for a variety of business types. Each practice file has a chart of accounts and items list for that particular type of business. This is a great way to see how to set up different types of businesses and how the transactions are recorded. (It is also a good resource for standard chart of accounts and items list when setting up client files). You can explore the different sample company files to learn more about QuickBooks and how to set it up for different types of businesses.

With QuickBooks Premier Accountant edition, you will have the following sample company files available:

- Product based business

- Service based business

- Nonprofit organization

- Contractor business

- Manufacturing business

- Wholesale/distribution business

- Consulting business (that's you!)

- ▶ Engineering or architecture firm

- ▶ Graphic design or advertising agency

- ▶ Law firm

- ▶ Retailer who tracks summarized sales

- ▶ Retailer who tracks individual sales

Resources

Intuit provides many resources to accountants and ProAdvisors. You can get to these resources at <u>account-ant.intuit.com</u> and/or <u>qbadvisor.com</u>. Some of the resources you may find useful include:

- ▶ Training webinars, seminars, self-study and webcasts – there are numerous training resources at account-ant.intuit.com and many of them are free and available at your convenience.

"I would suggest spending time training yourself on additional QuickBooks, tips & tricks and certifications. Never stop. Knowledge is Power! Billable Power!"
Michael Peters, Abacus Rex, Lombard Illinois

- ▶ Community message boards – this is a great place to get your questions answered. It is also a good place to read the questions and answers posted.

"It is essential that you immerse your self in as much Quickbooks information as you can get your hands on. You never know when a client well have specific problem that you have heard about. Join the forums and absorb as much as you can."

▶ Articles – there are many articles available on a variety of topics including accounting, technology, practice development and tax issues. Many articles include resources and tools you may find useful such as checklists, sample letters, and more.

▶ Engagement letters and checklists – there are sample engagement letters that you can download and tailor for your business.

▶ Newsletter – the Intuit ProConnection newsletter keeps you up to date on changes or updates to QuickBooks, tips and tricks, special offers, and other important information. You will learn some things before the general public—such as release dates for the program, updates, and more. You can subscribe to the newsletter at accountant.intuit.com, under Practice Resources; ProConnection newsletter there is a link to sign up.

▶ The Sleeter Group also offers many tools and resources for accountants and a certification program for their consultants. Their website is www.sleeter.com and there is also "free stuff" available including a client interview form available for downloading. The Sleeter Group publishes several books and products that can help improve your knowledge base and grow your business. Their book QuickBooks Consultant's Reference Guide is a great resource and provides many tips, tricks, and workarounds.

"Learn as much as possible about the program; there are so many free and inexpensive ways to do this. You will be loved by your clients if you have a ready answer."

Gain Experience

Work for Another ProAdvisor

Before you start your own QuickBooks consulting business, you may find that you need more experience. You really need experience with QuickBooks consulting for different types of businesses. You need to know how different types of businesses operate and understand the procedures they use. If you don't have enough business experience or background, you need to get more experience before you go out on your own.

So the question becomes, how much experience do you need? It depends on what type of experience you are getting. You need experience with several different types of businesses and different types of consulting (set-up, problem solving, and training). If you can work with another QuickBooks ProAdvisor for a year or more, you may feel ready to go on your own. However, if you are working in a larger firm and only working with one or two types of clients, you may need several years to get the breadth of experience that you need.

"I started by working as a subcontractor to an accounting firm that offered QuickBooks training and support to its clients. Over time I developed my own clients, but still provide services to accounting firms who prefer to outsource this service than staff internally."

Working for another ProAdvisor can help you learn the ropes before you go on your own. You can improve your QuickBooks expertise as well as learn more about the business of consulting. By working for another ProAdvisor for a period of time, you can minimize potential mistakes and be more prepared when you start your own QuickBooks consulting business.

Volunteer for Non-Profits

Another way to improve your knowledge base and gain experience is to volunteer to help smaller non-profit organizations with its bookkeeping. Whether it is the PTA, Little League, Church, Scouts, or Home Owner's Association, there is probably an organization that would welcome your help. There are many organizations that could benefit if you would set up their books on QuickBooks and then use the program for their monthly bookkeeping. At some point, you could train a new treasurer to use QuickBooks for the bookkeeping. You would gain experience, help a non-profit organization, and be networking all at the same time. You should also ask the organization for a testimonial to use in marketing your business!

If the non-profit organization uses fund accounting, you may not have the qualifications necessary to help them. Fund accounting and the regulations surrounding directed donations, restricted funds, etc. are complex accounting issues. You should refer them to someone who specializes in non-profit organizations. If you need additional information, a great resource is the book *Running QuickBooks for Non-Profits* by Kathy Ivens.

Discount Initially

Sometimes it is hard to get the first few clients. Some consultants will discount their services to get started. If you want to do this, it is better to tell the clients that since you are just getting started you want to use them as a reference and testimonial. In exchange, you will offer them a discounted rate. If you do this, make sure the clients know what your normal billing rates will be and that you are giving them a discount. You do not want them to expect the discounted rate in the future or tell others about your lower rate!

"Learn the product really well. Don't get down on yourself if you don't know the answer. You can't possibly know the answer to every question a client can have. Get to know other advisors and join as many groups that have other advisors as you can. This way when you don't know the answer you can find someone who does. Don't ever negotiate on price. Clients who want to nickel and dime you are on the wrong side of the 80/20 rule. They will complain the most, suck up a ton of time and then not pay you."
Terri Wilson, Offcierge Inc., Cincinnati, OH

Chapter 5

Setting up Your Business

Once you have decided that you are ready to start you own QuickBooks consulting business, there are a lot of things to be done. This chapter discusses what you need to do to start your business.

Types of Entities

One of the first things you have to do when starting a business is to decide what type of entity is right for your business. The type of entity you choose depends on your personal financial situation as well as your business plans. The following is a general discussion of business entities but you should seek additional information (from an attorney or tax advisor) prior to making a final decision.

Keep in mind that the type of entity that is appropriate for you when you start your business may not be the right type of entity as the business grows. For example, until you reach a certain level of profitability, you will not benefit from some of the tax savings possible with an S Corporation. You might consider starting with the more basic entity types (sole proprietor or a limited liability company) during the early years and then reconsider as your business grows.

When selecting the type of entity for your business, some things to consider include:

► Liability protection – as a new, small business you would have to personally guarantee any liabilities of the business anyway.

► Complexity of creating, maintaining, and filing requirements—the types of entities are listed below from easiest
to more complex.

► Tax planning considerations—you have to reach a certain level of sales/income before you can take advantage
of some of the benefits.

► Image—some people just like the idea of being a "corporation" and think it portrays a better image for the
business.

The types of entities available for your business are generally:

► Sole Proprietor

► Limited Liability Company

► Partnership

► Corporation

► S-Corporation

When you are ready to create your entity, you have several options available to complete the required paperwork and
filing requirements with the state to legally form your business.
You may hire an attorney, use a company such as MyCorporation, or do it yourself. If you are forming the business with
someone else or have complex financial situations, then you
definitely should consult an attorney. If you are the only one
involved without complex issues, then you may consider using
Intuit's MyCorporation. MyCorporation (www.MyCorp.com) is a
GREAT, easy to use and affordable alternative to form an LLC
or corporation. Their website helps guide you through deciding
which type of entity is right for you based upon your personal
situation.

Steps to Getting Started

Federal ID Number

Once you have selected the type of entity for your business and a business name, then you need to get a Federal ID number (FEIN). Even if you are a sole proprietor with no employees, you should get a FEIN. It does not cost anything to obtain a FEIN and you do not want to use your social security number for business because of the risk of identity theft.

There are several ways to obtain a FEIN, but the easiest is to go to the IRS website (www.irs.gov). You can fill the form out online and you will have your FEIN in a matter of minutes. Then, the IRS will send the FEIN confirmation in the mail. Remember the IRS does not charge to get a FEIN! If you accidentally go to www.irs.com instead of www.irs.gov they will ask for your credit card number and charge you $19.95 for a FEIN! So, be careful to type in the correct website.

Bank Account and Credit Card

Now that you have your entity type and FEIN, you can open a business checking account. You want to make sure to keep your business and personal accounts separate, so open another checking account.

Many banks now offer free checking accounts to small businesses so be sure to shop around for the best banking package. If possible, select a bank that works with QuickBooks so that you can get experience with online banking. You can learn about downloading transactions and paying bills online using QuickBooks. This is an area that clients will ask about!

You may also want to get a credit card to use for business purposes. Again, you should always keep business and personal charges separate. Although you can get the credit card in the business name, you will most likely still be personally liable for any charges.

Business Licenses and Permits

As a business, you may need to obtain a business license from your city, county and/or state. You can contact city hall where the business will be located to ask about the local requirements. You can also contact your local Small Business Development Center (SBDC) for help in determining what licenses and permits you will need.

Insurance

As a business, you need to examine your insurance needs and coverage. Our society has become very litigious and you need to protect yourself. It may seem like you are not vulnerable since you are providing only consulting services. But, what if your client's computer crashes right after you were there working on their QuickBooks file? What if it costs them thousands of dollars for data recovery? What if they cannot ship anything for several days? It may not have been your fault, but you should have insurance to protect yourself in case of a lawsuit.

You should talk with an insurance agent about insurance for errors and omissions, business equipment, business use of your automobile, home office, clients coming to your home, and many other topics. You should also investigate business interruption insurance if this is your sole source of income. If your current insurance agent does not handle business clients, you should find another agent for your business insurance needs.

Set Up Your Office

Whether you decide to have a home office or an outside office, you will need a dedicated place to work. Having a home office is much more accepted today than it was ten years ago and it can save you a considerable amount of money in overhead expenses. A QuickBooks consulting business does not require that you have a physical office to meet with clients. Most of the time, you will meet clients at their place of business. If your client also has a home office, you can find another place to meet such as a coffee shop or library room.

In addition, remote access gives you the ability to access clients' computers remotely. The basic remote access is included with QuickBooks Premier Accountant Edition for the first year. Remote access makes it even easier to have a home office and saves you travel time!

Business Phone Line

It is more professional to have a dedicated phone line and answering machine. Instead of using a basic answering machine, you may want to have an answering service answer your calls when you are not available.

You may choose to use your cell phone number as your business number. If you do this, you should not take calls during client appointments unless it is an emergency. If you do need to leave your phone on during a client meeting, make sure you let the client know the situation up front and assure them that they will not be charged for any time you are on the phone.

Software Required

Software required was discussed in Chapter 3 in the section on Start-up costs. As a review, you will obviously need QuickBooks Premier Accountant Edition for the current year and previous years (at least three years).

You also should have Microsoft Office, and you must have Internet security and anti-virus software. It seems like the opinions on which works best changes frequently, so you should read software reviews to help you select which one to use.

In addition to software, you also need a good, reliable, automatic back up system in place. Your business is dependent upon your computer and protecting your data is critical. In addition to backing up critical files locally, you should consider QuickBooks online backup solution mentioned previously. It is affordable, secure, reliable, and comforting to know you do not have to worry about losing critical data.

Website and E-mail

A website is an absolutely necessity if you want to present a professional business image. Potential clients need to be able to go to your website to assess your credibility and determine whether they want to do business with you or not. The good news is that creating and hosting a website is a lot easier and more affordable than it used to be.

There are many companies that provide affordable web hosting services. For example, GoDaddy.com, NetworkSolutions.com, Netfirms.com, and even Yahoo are just a few of firms to consider. You can get a decent website hosted for as little as $5 a month that provides ten email addresses and adequate storage space for most consultants. If you are a ProAdvisor, you can get a free, three page website from Homestead for twelve months. If you start small, you can always increase your hosting package as your website grows.

You should explore the domain names that are available for your website and take that into consideration when choosing your company name. You should really try to have your business name and website domain name be the same or as close as possible. If possible, you should also choose a domain name with ".com" since that is the most common extension.

Having your own email address helps establish credibility and professionalism. Think about the image you present as a consultant that uses free emails such as Yahoo, Hotmail, etc. Having an email address of <u>John123@hotmail.com</u>, for example, does not present a good image for your business as a consultant. Unless you have a great QuickBooks related name, you should not use these email addresses. You will present a more professional image with an email associated with your own website, such as 'john@johnconsultant.com.'

Usually the web hosting firm also provides software or templates for creating your own website. You no longer need to know HTML to create a professional looking website. If you can use Publisher and/or PowerPoint, then you can probably create your own website. It is important that the website present the image you want for your business. You do not want a website with misspellings or that will reflect poorly on the image you wish to project. If you cannot do it yourself, then hire someone to do it for you. A bad website is worse than no website at all!

See Chapter 8 on Marketing for additional discussion about websites and what makes a good or bad website.

Equipment, Furniture, and Supplies

As a consultant, you will need traditional office equipment and supplies and you may already have much of what you will need. You should have the following:

- ▶ Computer, back up system, and surge protection

- ▶ Flash, Jump or USB drives and/or CDs for data storage

- ▶ Printer/scanner/copier (possibly a fax, although scanning and attaching the image to an email is becoming more popular)

- ▶ Shredder (security and confidentiality of client information is of utmost importance)

- ▶ Telephone, answering machine and cell phone – you may choose to go totally wireless and use one cell phone number as your business number.

- ▶ High speed Internet service

- ▶ Optional – Desk, chair, file cabinet(s), bookshelves and credenza(s)

- ▶ Copier paper and toner or ink

- ▶ Paper, pens and pencils

Write a Business Plan

A written business plan is always a good idea when starting a business. The process of writing the plan involves a lot of research and consideration of various factors that will help in starting your business successfully. Software and courses (or seminars) are available that will help you develop a business plan.

Perhaps the best, hands-on business development program is the Kauffman Foundation's FastTrac™ New Venture course which is offered nationally through organizations, community colleges, and universities. This course not only assists you with writing a business plan (complete with three years projected financial statements), but you most likely also will develop a great networking group and contacts. For additional information about FastTrac™ and their business development programs visit www.fasttrac.org or www.kauffman.org.

Chapter 6

Financial Matters

If you are a QuickBooks consultant, then it is assumed that you are familiar with financial matters. Therefore, the following discussion of financial considerations of starting your own consulting business will be brief.

Create a Budget

It is wise to create a three year budget to determine your income and cash requirements. You need to make sure you will have adequate funds available for the business as well as personal requirements.

Project Income

As you project your income, you should be realistic in how quickly you will acquire new clients. As a consultant, your business will grow primarily as a result of referrals and relationships which take time to develop. So, the first few months and year should reflect slow and modest growth. The second year will most likely grow at a somewhat faster pace and the third year even more. Do not assume rapid growth—be realistic.

There is also some seasonality to QuickBooks consulting. During the first few months of the year (through May), clients want to get set up on QuickBooks and start using it for the new year. Usually the summer months are not too busy, with work limited to more troubleshooting clients and new businesses. During the fall, business will increase again with clients trying to clean up their books for year end.

Also, keep in mind that a good number of your hours will be spent on non-billable activities. You will spend time on administrative matters and networking events. Especially when you are starting your business, you need to allocate considerable time to attending meetings and events for networking and building relationships for referrals. Some estimate that 30-50% of your time is spent on non-billable activities.

Expenses

If you plan on starting alone with a home office, then your monthly business expenses will be minimal. You should still budget for annual expenses such as membership fees for the QuickBooks ProAdvisor Program, Chamber of Commerce, association dues, other software updates, business licenses, insurance premiums and other expenses. Remember owners draws are not considered an expense, but include them in cash outflows.

Estimated Taxes

Unless you are an employee getting a W-2 from the business, you most likely will have to pay estimated tax payments quarterly. You need to make estimate tax payments if you are a sole-proprietor, partner, LLC member, or S-Corporation owner, and you expect to owe tax of over $1,000 when you file your return. Make sure you have the funds available to make these quarterly payments and include estimates in your cash flow budget.

Also, do not forget the self-employment tax (FICA and Medicare) which is essentially 15.3% of your self-employment income. The self-employment tax is paid as part of your estimate taxes quarterly.

It is important that you keep your own business's financial statements current so that you can estimate your net income for calculating the estimate tax payments due. Also, set aside money regularly so you have adequate funds available to make the quarterly estimated tax payments. As a rule of thumb, save a third of your gross income in a separate savings account or money market so that you do not spend it!

Keep Business and Personal Separate

One of the first things you should do when setting up your new business is to open a business checking account and/or credit card. It is important to keep your personal finances separate from business activity. If you pay for business expenses with a personal check or credit card, you should have the business reimburse you from the business' checking account. Pretend that you are an employee and turn in your receipts and reimburse yourself with a check from the business account.

Keep in mind that unless you are an employee getting a W-2 from your business, the money you take out of the business is considered "Owners Draws" or "Disbursements". It is not a business expense. Also, do not pay for your personal expenses from the business' checking account or credit card. Instead, take a draw from the business and pay personal expenses from your personal accounts.

Manage Cash Flows – Billing and Collecting

If you do not always collect money when you deliver the service, then you need to stay on top of invoicing clients. You should use QuickBooks to email the invoices to your clients. This not only saves you money (toner or ink, paper, envelope, and postage), but it should result in you getting paid sooner. The invoice should include payment terms, i.e, net 10 days.

If a client has not paid you within the specified payment terms, you should not hesitate to send a reminder invoice. You need to demonstrate good collection procedures if you expect your clients to do the same in their businesses. If you are not getting paid, then you should not continue working for the client.

Accept Credit Cards

You may find that some clients want to pay with a credit card. If your volume is large enough, you should consider signing up for a merchant service (QuickBooks Merchant Service). However, if you only need to accept a credit card payment periodically, you can have your clients pay you using PayPal. Obviously you will need to set up a PayPal account. You should also realize that the PayPal fees to accept a credit card are 3-4%, but there are no monthly fees or other requirements (like some merchant accounts). Whether you charge the client for the extra fee or not is up to you, but sometimes accepting credit card payments allows you to get paid sooner.

Tax Considerations

As a business, there may be some tax advantages that you can utilize. You should research and analyze which are right for you. Some considerations include the home office deduction, hiring your children or spouse to work for the business, retirement plans, medial savings accounts and more. As your business grows, these considerations become more important and should be reconsidered. For example, you may not need or be able to contribute to a SIMPLE IRA during the first couple of years. However, as the business grows you should consider tax saving strategies.

Mileage and Other Expenses

You need to track your mileage and have the business reimburse you for the mileage periodically. If the business cannot reimburse you for the mileage, you should record a due to owner to get the expense on the books. Obviously, you need to track mileage to and from clients. You should also record mileage to the bank for deposits, to the office supply store, to any seminars you take or conduct, and any other business related miles.

Chapter 7

Define Your Services and Billing Rates

Usually one of the hardest parts about starting your own consulting business is defining the services you will offer and setting your billing rates. New consultants tend to want to offer any and all services—they need clients and work. New consultants also tend to under estimate the value of the services they offer and thus set their billing rates too low. Hopefully, the information in this chapter will help you clearly identify the services you will offer and set appropriate billing rates.

Services Provided

As a new consultant, you need to clearly identify the services you will provide. It may be tempting to say that you will do anything and everything, but this is not a good idea. You need to focus your time and efforts on a few services that you can provide and manage with a good level of quality. For example, if you are operating your business alone, can you really stay current on all the tax law changes for all types of entities as well as maintain and expand your QuickBooks knowledge base and all the programs and features offered? Identify the services you will provide and develop referrals or sub-contractors to provide the other services.

"Maybe..not to try to do so much right away. I think I've tried to do too much in my first year. I marketed bookkeeping, payroll, training, support, all aspects of QB consulting, as well as 3rd party integration. I am now pulling back and decreasing my focus. I will widen my focus more slowly as I grow and can afford support staff."

Based on the National Survey of QuickBooks ProAdvisors (see Appendix A), the most common services provided in addition to QuickBooks consulting are:

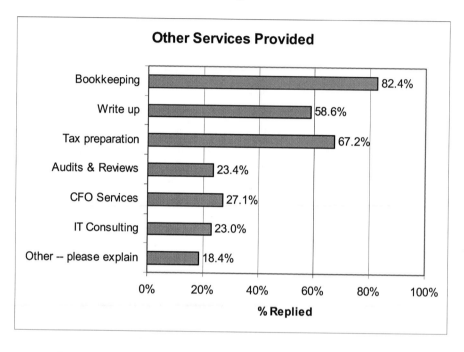

Other Services Provided

Service	% Replied
Bookkeeping	82.4%
Write up	58.6%
Tax preparation	67.2%
Audits & Reviews	23.4%
CFO Services	27.1%
IT Consulting	23.0%
Other -- please explain	18.4%

As you can see, bookkeeping, write up and tax preparation are the most common other services offered in addition to QuickBooks consulting. Less than one-fourth offer audits and review, or IT consulting due to the level of expertise required for those services.

"Do taxes and bookkeeping too. They are natural fits with QuickBooks consulting and provide a lot of referral business."

Intuit's Annual Billing Rate Survey

Each year, Intuit surveys subscribers to the Intuit Pro-Connection newsletter about their billing rates and practices. There are several articles discussing the results of the survey available at accountant.intuit.com. The articles can be found by going to: Practice Resources, Intuit ProConnection, Articles, and they are dated May 18, 2007. Some results from the survey have been included in this chapter, and more details can be found in Appendix B.

A few consultants list their billing rates on their website especially if they charge fixed fees. However, if you really need and want to find out billing rates of competitors, you might consider emailing another ProAdvisor in a different city, i.e., not a direct competitor. Many consultants are willing to help and answer your questions, especially if you are not located where you would be a likely competitor.

Personal Credentials and Expertise

If you have a lot of credentials and expertise, your billing rate should reflect your background and experience. If you have gone to college, passed the CPA exam, and obtained the work experience to become a licensed CPA, your billing rates should reflect this knowledge and expertise. Similarly, if you are a bookkeeper who has earned a certification from a national bookkeeping association, your billing rates should reflect that.

If you are going to be a QuickBooks consultant, you need to earn the Certified QuickBooks ProAdvisor designation. You also should strive to earn the other certifications offered for QuickBooks Point of Sale and QuickBooks Enterprise Edition. By earning the certifications, you demonstrate a level of knowledge that clients expect and you differentiate yourself (see the chart in Chapter 8 on percent of ProAdvisors that earn various certifications). However, you also need some practical, hands-on experience as well.

Do not be afraid to set your billing rates to reflect your credentials and expertise. Clients have different levels of complexities and needs, and they will choose the consultant that will meet their needs. For example, a client that operates a service business alone may not need a high powered consultant with the highest billing rates; whereas a manufacturing business that has inventory in multiple warehouses may need a consultant with more expertise. In addition, if you decide to use different billing rates depending on the client, QuickBooks allows you to specify which price level applies to the client.

Intuit's 2007 Rates Survey provides details of rates charged based on designations (bookkeeper, CPA, Certified ProAdvisor, etc.). See Appendix B for more information on billing rates by designation and the link to the articles. This is the general chart for average bookkeeping rate charged by designation:

Designation	Bookkeeping Rate
Bookkeepers*	$48
All ProAdvisors Who Are Not CPAs	$53
QuickBooks ProAdvisors (Uncertified)	$59
All QuickBooks ProAdvisors	**$60**
Certified QuickBooks ProAdvisors	$60
All Respondents	$61
All ProAdvisors Who Are CPAs	$68
CPAs	$71

*This category does not include CPAs or QuickBooks ProAdvisors.

As this chart shows, the billing rates increase with certifications and credentials. Keep in mind that these are basic bookkeeping billing rates, not consulting rates. Refer to the article (mentioned above) from the Intuit ProConnection newsletter (on the website accountant.intuit.com) for additional billing rates by designation.

Local Market

Rural vs. City

As you would expect, billing rates in urban areas tend to be higher than other areas. An article based on the 2007 Intuit Rates Survey reports bookkeeping billing rates by population density. (see Appendix B for complete reference). Following is the general overview of bookkeeping rates based on population density from the article:

Density	Count	Range	Average	Mode
National	750	$10-$180	$61	$50
Rural (Sparse)	34	$25-$125	$54	$50
Semi-Rural	98	$17-$130	$54	$50
Suburban	229	$10-$180	$61	$50
Mid-sized City	217	$10-$175	$60	$60
Urban (Dense)	158	$20-$160	$71	$50
Nonlocal	14	$30-$115	$60	$75

Competition – Other ProAdvisors

Another consideration when setting your billing rates is the competition. If there are a lot of ProAdvisors in your area, the competition will be greater and the pressure to maintain competitive billing rates will be more intense. You need to analyze your credentials and expertise in comparison to your competitors. If your expertise and background is greater than the competition, then do not hesitate to charge a billing rate that reflects your credentials. However, be prepared to market your credentials.

Often, new consultants set their billing rates low in an effort to gain new clients quickly. This is not a good idea for several reasons. If your billing rates are lower than other ProAdvisors, then clients may assume that you are not as qualified. The other problem is that it is hard to increase your billing rates once you have set them.

"I didn't charge a high enough rate in the beginning. I now charge travel time to clients who are more than 10 miles away or so. I also now have a 2-hour minimum. This year, I plan to require my older clients to upgrade to newer versions of QuickBooks at least every two or three years -I'm still supporting people who have QuickBooks 3.0!! But not for much longer..."

You should also not set your billing rates low simply because you have a home office and lower overhead costs. You can provide quality services to clients whether you have a home office or an expensive office somewhere else. Your billing rates should be based on your credentials and expertise, not where your office is located.

Client Considerations

Different clients will present different levels of complexity and difficulty. For example, accounting for a small service based business involving only the owner is easier than accounting for a manufacturing or retail business with inventory issues. In addition, clients will have different levels of bookkeeping knowledge and experience which will affect how much time and attention is required. Some clients are more self reliant than others which can allow you to perform higher level consulting or troubleshooting services.

Your billing rates also will impact the types of clients that you acquire. If you have high billing rates, small service based business may not be able to afford your services. However, if your high billing rates are due to your credentials and expertise, you should be working with the more complex clients.

Services Provided

When setting your billing rates, you should also consider the types of services you provide. Many consultants start out as generalists working with all types of clients and industries. However, as your business and expertise grows, you should consider specializing in a type of client or industry or services provided. For example, Dawn Scranton, a Certified QuickBooks ProAdvisor, specializes in integrating third-party add-on software. When you specialize, you are able to charge a higher billing rate for your expertise. In fact, Dawn reported that her income tripled after she specialized. You can read the interview with Dawn in Appendix D or listen or download it from www.mlongconsulting.com.

In the National Survey of QuickBooks ProAdvisors (see Appendix A), the consultants who replied reported that they specialize in the following industries:

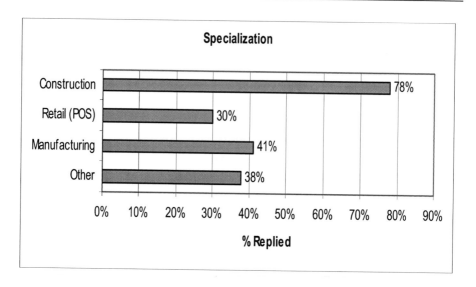

Some of the 'Other' specialties most frequently mentioned are: Services, Non-Profits, Medical/Health care, real estate, and more. When choosing an area for your specialty, you should consider your interests, prior experience, the types of local businesses or industries, as well as competitive ProAdvisors and their specialties.

Hourly vs. Fixed Fee

Accounting and bookkeeping services traditionally have been billed by hourly rates and many consultants still use hourly billing rates. As a new consultant, you should consider the pros and cons to determine which is right for you. First, lets consider how some QuickBooks consultants are using fixed fee billing in their practices.

Packaged or Pre-paid Services

Some consultants are setting fixed fees for "packages" of their services that they generally post on their websites (with the prices). The following are examples of some packages offered by QuickBooks consultants:

- Custom installation and set-up of new data file

- Quarterly tune-up or maintenance

- Quarterly phone support for X number of hours (discounted somewhat from normal billing rates)

- Phone support – X amount for 15 minutes (with a minimum charge)

- On-site training – half day or full day

Pros and Cons – Hourly

As a new consultant, you may have a difficult time trying to determine how long performing or completing different services will take. It is often hard to estimate the time involved until you actually look into clients' data files and assess the situation. Billing by the hour ensures that you will get paid for all the time you work.

However, clients often are anxious and concerned since they do not know how much it is going to cost with hourly billing. Sometimes they will be watching the clock and you will feel rushed or pressured to do the work quickly. However, it may be in the clients' best interest for you to take your time and do quality work rather than rushing the work. Clients may also hesitate to call with questions if they are worried about it being on the clock.

Pros and Cons – Fixed Fee

As a consultant, you may actually earn more per hour with fixed fee arrangements. If you have standard company files for different types of businesses (service, retail, contractor, etc.) it will not take long to customize for a particular client. The client does not know how long you spend on it; they only know the fixed fee. So, you may be able to charge a fixed fee of say $250 for "new file set up and customization" and it may only take you 30 minutes to do the work.

Other Considerations

Discounts – initially and/or non-profits

When you are starting your new consulting business, you are anxious to get work and new clients. As a result, many new consultants are tempted to offer a low billing rate just to get the work. If you do this, you should do it the right way. For example, you can tell the client what your normal billing rate is, but you will provide them with a discount in exchange for their testimonial to use on your website. You should also let them know that in the future, you will charge your normal billing rates. You do not want clients to expect the lower billing rate to continue indefinitely, nor do you want them to refer new clients to you expecting the lower billing rate.

"I didn't charge enough for a long time. It took me a while to catch up because I couldn't reasonably increase my hourly rate to existing clients by large sums! Also, I think I was (still can be) overly generous with my time."
Debbi C. Warden, CPA, MBA, The Business Manager, LLC
Centennial, CO

You may choose to offer a discount to small non-profit organizations. This is a good way to support and give back to your community. You may also make contacts and get referrals as a result of the work you do for them. If the organization has a newsletter, you might consider doing the work for free in exchange for recognition or ad space in their newsletter or on their website. Thus, you are helping the organization and getting some exposure for your business as well. However, if the non-profit organization uses fund accounting, make sure you have the required expertise or refer the non-profit to another ProAdvisor with the appropriate expertise!

Billable vs. non-billable time

Keep in mind that not all of your time working is billable time. You will spend a good number of hours on non-billable activities. During the early years of your consulting business, you should spend a considerable amount of time attending meetings and events for networking and building relationships for referrals. It is not uncommon to have 30-50% of your time spent on non-billable activities. These activities are crucial to growing your business though. It is crucial to continually market and network to keep your business growing, even when you are busy with billable time!

"Get involved in your community. I joined the local Chamber of Commerce and although I have only received 2 clients through the Chamber, I have been able to make many contacts. Currently, I serve as the Treasurer for the Chamber."

Chapter 8

Marketing – Initial Considerations

There is more to marketing than simply advertising. Marketing encompasses your product or service, price, place, and promotions. Previous chapters discussed defining your services, setting your billing rates, and setting up your office. This chapter discusses some initial marketing considerations and Chapter 9 discusses promotional and marketing methods for consultants.

Develop Your Identity

As you start your new consulting business, you should consider what image you want for your business, because that will impact everything else related to marketing your services. How do you want people to describe and think about your business? Explore other ProAdvisors websites for ideas on positioning your consulting business.

For example, do you want to emphasize that you have the lowest rates? Do you offer 24 hour service? Do you have specialized expertise? What do you want to emphasize? Will that attract the types of clients that you are targeting?

Since you are selling services, you are really selling yourself. You should strive for an image that will instill confidence and trust in your abilities and expertise.

Name

You will need to select a name for your new business and this can be challenging. You should try to select a name that is also available as a domain name for your website. Brainstorm as many possible names as you can come up with. Then, go to the website for your secretary of state and search business names to see which names are available in your state. You should also search domain names (via GoDaddy, Netfirms, or other web hosting companies) to see what is available. Choosing a name is hard and takes some time. Ask other people for their ideas and suggestions as well.

Website

As discussed previously, you need a professional looking website. When you are exploring the websites of other ProAdvisors, make notes about what you like and do not like about the website. Look at the website from the perspective of a potential client—what impression would they get from the website?

Some ProAdvisors' websites are only three pages long and not very impressive. Other websites appear loud and cheesy with numerous "Save Now" or "Buy Here" links and buttons. They appear to be desperately trying to sell you some-thing—QuickBooks, checks and forms, e-books, online seminars, and anything else you might be willing to pay for. If you have links for QuickBooks products at a discount, have a separate tab for "products" and include it all on one page—not every page and definitely not your home page!

So what makes a good website? Include a picture(s) of yourself (it helps with credibility) and have an "about us" page with your credentials and experience. Include client testimonials or a client list to instill confidence in your abilities. Do not have lots of text since no one will read it. Use bullet point lists in-stead. Do not just list the services you provide. Instead, focus on the benefits your services will provide—how will you help solve their problems?

See Chapter 5 for more detailed information about setting up a website with a hosting company.

Business cards

Your business card is just as important as your website. You do not want to print your own or have cheap flimsy cards. Again, what image do you want to project for your business?

Your business card is like a mini-billboard for your business. Obviously you need to include your contact information such as you name, address, phone number(s), email, and website address. People know what an email and web address look like so it is not necessary to label them. You do not need to put **email**: john123@hotmail.com. Simply show the email address. If you have a home office, you might consider using a post office box instead of your home address.

Do not forget that there are two sides to your cards. It does not cost much more to use the back side as well. Your business card is also a marketing piece for your business. You can list some of the services you provide on the back of the card and/or a slogan. Again, your business card should not be too cluttered and it needs to portray the right image for your business.

You can get great quality cards relatively inexpensive from online printers. Overnightprints.com and Vistaprints.com are some vendors.

Analyze Competitors

You should spend some time analyzing the other ProAdvisors in your area as well as other areas. Check out their profiles and certifications on the Find-a-ProAdvisor website. Also, go to their website and learn more about their businesses. Are they specializing in a certain industry or type of client? Does their website and profile present a good, favorable image or not? What other services do they offer?

How will your business compare to the competition? How will you try to differentiate yourself from them? You can specialize by type of client or industry. Maybe you want to specialize in third party add-on integrations or just one or two add-on programs. Will you be available nights and weekends? Try to find a way to make yourself different than the other ProAdvisors.

"I learned from someone else's advice and maybe someone can learn by my adding this to our "advice column". Try to differentiate yourself from others. For example, your first hour of QuickBooks consulting for a new client can be free. Also, always remember to inform your prospective new client of your ProAdvisor discount on ordering software and supplies."
Mary P. Harris, Harris Accounting and Bookkeeping, Bel Air, MD

One way to differentiate yourself is by earning Intuit's Certifications. There are over 40,000 people who have joined the QuickBooks ProAdvisor Program. However, only a small percentage of those ProAdvisors earn the various certifications. As the chart shows, only 37% of the ProAdvisors become Certified ProAdvisors. That is surprising, and even fewer obtain the other certifications available.

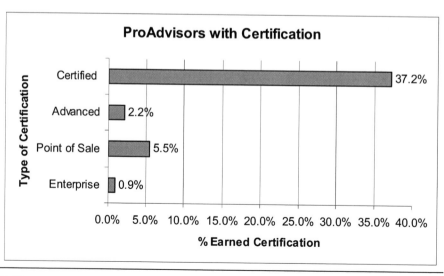

Define the Target Market

What type of clients will you target? You need to have a clear idea of your ideal client so that you can target them in your marketing efforts. You also need to be able to tell others what type of client you are looking for so that they can provide referrals to you. It is not enough to simply say "small businesses". You need to be more precise. When defining your target market, consider these questions about the business or organization:

▶ What stage is the business in – start up, growth, mature

▶ Number of employees and annual revenue

▶ Types of products or services they provide

▶ Liberal or conservative

▶ Environment-friendly

▶ Employee / family - friendly

▶ Fast growing / adopt new ideas

▶ Type of employees – younger, education level, full or part time

▶ Company culture and management style

Now that you've identified your company image and your target market, you will need to focus on specific marketing methods.

Chapter 9

Marketing – Methods

Just because you have started your business does not mean clients will seek your services. Virtually every consultant has to engage in marketing to get clients and grow their business. Because you are selling a service (therefore yourself), traditional marketing methods are not as effective. This chapter discusses marketing methods other than your own website.

Find-a-ProAdvisor Website

If you join QuickBooks ProAdvisor Program and become a Certified QuickBooks ProAdvisor, you will be listed on the Find-a-ProAdvisor website. This is a great source of referrals for many consultants. However, if there are several ProAdvisors nearby, it may take awhile for your name to be listed on the first page. ProAdvisors who have earned the Advanced Certification are listed first, and you need to have been certified for three years before you can earn the Advanced Certification. So, it may take some time before you see many referrals from this website, but 30,000 people visit the website per month! Intuit markets this website extensively, including (new for 2008) inside QuickBooks itself (on the help menu)!

"The first thing you must do is complete your website set up (Find-a-ProAdvisor profile). I get most of my referrals from the Quickbooks (Find-a-ProAdvisor) website."
Brad Lee White Sr., BW Consulting. Brooklyn, NY.

Regardless, you should have a good profile on the website. This is another place where potential clients evaluate you and your credibility. Review the profiles of other ProAdvisors and note things that potential clients would look for. You should consider posting your picture on the profile and take the time to completely fill out the profile. You can also provide a link to your website and your email address. You should provide as much information as possible and make it easy for potential clients to reach you. You also need to convey your credibility and expertise.

"Keep your website (profile) updated, people really look at it, no matter how many consultants they see, you never know what a client is looking for, they could be looking for you."

Write Articles

A great method to help build credibility is to write articles. If you can write articles for the local newspaper, small business publication, newsletters, or websites, you can help build your reputation as an expert. Look for publications that your target market of potential clients might read so they will see your article. If you write the article, the publisher or editor usually will include a couple of sentences about you and your business at the end of the article. This is free marketing for your business and many local publications are looking for free material to publish.

You should also post all your articles on your website. Potential clients then can see and read articles that you have written and have been published. It helps build your credibility and expertise. If you cannot get published, write the articles for your own website or newsletter!

Conduct Seminars

A great marketing method is to conduct QuickBooks or other small business seminars. Teaching the seminar helps build your credibility and expertise. You should not use the seminars to "sell" yourself, but you should always bring your business cards. If you merely introduce yourself and give your elevator pitch (one minute about your business and services you provide), attendees usually will ask for your card if they are interested in your services. Conducting seminars is a great source of new clients and referrals.

You do not have to sponsor or conduct seminars by yourself. Try to get involved with the local Small Business Development Center (SBDC), women's business center, chamber of commerce or other organizations as a seminar presenter for them. These organizations often offer seminars frequently and can provide the marketing and administration for the seminar while you present it. You may get paid only a small fee, but the real benefit is that you are networking, promoting your business, and building your credibility.

"I built my practice doing local seminars. Tripled the year I did this. This is very time consuming, but you can break even. I suggest the Sleeter materials and their 'Train the Trainer' seminar."

Intuit even provides customizable training resources (free) available for downloading on the ProAdvisor website (www.qbadvisor.com) in the new "Train Your Clients Center." They provide instructor's guide, presentation, and student handbook for seminars on QuickBooks Pro, QuickBooks Point of Sale, QuickBooks Premier for Contractors, and Simple Start. The "Train the Trainer" section has numerous free resources as well!

Referrals

As a consultant, a large part of your business may come from referrals. You should cultivate and seek referrals from everyone. Current clients are a great source of referrals, so do not forget to let them know that you always appreciate referrals. Some consultants are brave enough to ask clients for the names of other businesses that would benefit from their services.

"Referrals are the cornerstone of my business. Also patience...if a prospective client doesn't go with you at first, they eventually will. If a client uses you, chances are you'll get another call a few months down the road."

You can also seek referrals from other accountants, bankers, lawyers, chamber members, church members, soccer moms, friends, family, and almost anyone. You should always have business cards available and let other people know about your business. You need to be able to quickly explain the types of services you provide and the types of clients you serve so that when you meet someone who may be able to provide referrals, you are ready and know what to say.

"If you are a QuickBooks Consultant and not an accountant, the best way to grow your client base is to partner with accounting, legal and financial professionals where both parties can refer business to the other."
Vincent F. Triolo, Small Biz Assist, Allentown, PA

Getting referrals takes time to cultivate the relationship and earn the trust and respect of the person providing the referral. You should always acknowledge any referrals that you get and thank the person who provided the referral. If someone tells you that you should contact a potential client, you should follow though and make the contact. You should try to reciprocate referrals whenever possible as well.

Networking

You need to network to build contacts and your referral sources. You can network at the local Chamber of Commerce or any number of groups and organizations. You should always have plenty of business cards available for these events. Remember to listen as much or more than you talk—it is not all about you!

"Networking and building alliances within the local chamber or other local group and specializing in a specific industry such as retailing, auto"

Volunteer your time for local non-profit organizations and get involved in the activities or on the boards. Helping the PTA, Scouts, Church, Little League, or Home Owners Association can also be a networking opportunity for your business. As you meet members of these organizations and get to know them, you will build relationships that may provide referrals. Small business owners are everywhere and you do not always realize it. You should also remember your business image and that you are always representing your business at these events as well.

Ads in Newsletters

You may find that placing ads in the newsletters of local organizations is beneficial and usually the cost is not significant. If you are a member of the organization or a local resident, it may be even more effective. Some newsletters you might consider include:

- ▶ Home Owners' Association

- ▶ Church

- ▶ Parent Teacher Association or Organization

- ▶ Parks and Recreation program

Sponsorships

The number of kids playing soccer, football, baseball, and other sports activities continues to grow. Often, the Little Leagues are looking for sponsors to help with the costs. As a sponsor, you can have your company name and logo on the shirts or fields. This can also help spur conversations at the events where you can do some networking!

One small business owner in Lee's Summit, MO discovered a great way to sponsor a lot of teams while saving money. He approached the Little League and offered to sponsor all the teams that did not get another sponsor for around $1,000 which was far less than sponsoring each team for $300 since there were around 20 teams left. So, on Saturday afternoons at the soccer field, there was a ton of kids with his company logo on their shirts! Often the kids would wear the shirts to the store or out to eat providing even more exposure for his business.

Less Effective Methods

As a consultant, you are selling services and yourself. Not all marketing methods are as effective as some so think about how your clients would find and choose a consultant.

Trade Shows

If you are considering a booth at a trade show, you might reconsider. The cost of the booth alone is just the beginning. You also will need to have displays and props to make your booth inviting, which may cost another two to three times the initial booth fee. You also will need some freebies or prizes to give away to entice people to stop at your booth so you have a chance to talk with them. Usually you do not actually meet many people who are really potential clients. This is not a cost effective method of marketing for most QuickBooks consultants.

Traditional Ads

As a consultant, you are selling services and your own credibility and expertise. Clients do not normally choose a consultant based on traditional ads such as newspapers or magazines or commercials on television or radio. These methods of advertising are very expensive and not effective for most QuickBooks consultants.

"We wasted a lot of time and money on Brochures and Advertising that generally speaking did not pay off. However, you have to start somewhere, until referrals start coming in."
Paulette Dreher, SBS Associates, Inc., Westwood, NJ

National Survey Results

In the National Survey of ProAdvisors, consultants were asked what marketing methods they had used and how effective were the various methods. The responses are given in the charts below.

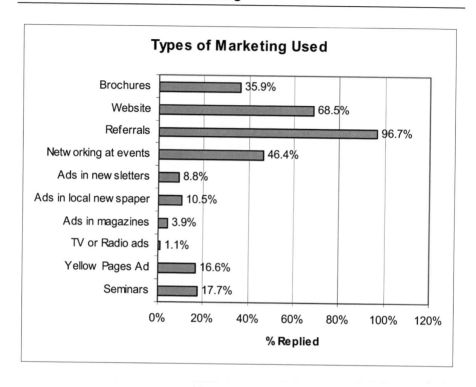

Types of Marketing Used

Type	% Replied
Brochures	35.9%
Website	68.5%
Referrals	96.7%
Networking at events	46.4%
Ads in newsletters	8.8%
Ads in local newspaper	10.5%
Ads in magazines	3.9%
TV or Radio ads	1.1%
Yellow Pages Ad	16.6%
Seminars	17.7%

	Very Effective	Somewhat Effective	Somewhat Ineffective	Very Ineffective
Brochures	6.5%	50.6%	28.6%	14.3%
Website	26.2%	47.5%	18.9%	7.4%
Referrals	79.8%	16.7%	2.4%	1.2%
Networking	22.1%	53.7%	18.9%	5.3%
Ads in newsletters	3.7%	18.5%	44.4%	33.3%
Ads in local newspaper	0.0%	21.9%	37.5%	40.6%
Ads in magazines	0.0%	16.7%	38.9%	44.4%
TV or Radio ads	0.0%	23.1%	38.5%	38.5%
Yellow Pages ad	7.0%	51.2%	14.0%	27.9%
Seminars	43.9%	31.7%	22.0%	2.4%

The responses provided by the consultants clearly demonstrate the importance and effectiveness of referrals.

Also, notice that very few consultants use traditional ads and those methods were generally rated as ineffective. So, it makes more sense to spend your marketing money on joining and attending networking events and luncheons than on placing ineffective ads.

Chapter 10

Performing the Engagement

You should develop some policies and procedures about how you will operate your consulting business. Intuit's website (accountant.intuit.com under the Practice Resources section) has several tools and articles for you to download that will help you build and grow your business. They also offer various seminars and/or webinars about providing excellent service and simplifying your workflow.

Client Interview

When you have a new client, completing an interview form can help start the relationship off right. The interview can allow you to get an overview of the business and their needs, and the form also helps make sure you do not forget to ask an important question. The completed interview form is also a useful reference to refer back to as needed.

You can use a fairly brief initial interview form during your first conversation with potential clients. This helps guide your conversation and allows you to document your conversation for future reference.

Then, you can have a more extensive interview form for actual clients. You can create your own interview form, use a generic template, or customize one for your use. In the Advanced Certification Course "Expert QuickBooks Consulting: In Pursuit of Service Excellence" there is a sample client interview form that is very detailed and extensive (10 pages long). This may be more than you need, so you could modify it to meet your needs.

"In the QuickBooks Accountant Update seminar last November 2006, they stated that QuickBooks consultants should get as much information as possible before a visit. (and provided information of suggested questions to ask.) Pay attention to that process because the more you know of the client the more prepared you will appear to the client, which can secure an on-going clent/ relationship."

Whatever interview form you decided to use, you should get in the habit of using an interview form with clients. It ensures that you ask all the pertinent questions, ensures that you listen to the answers, and provides documentation for future reference. As you grow and gain more clients, you may need to refer to your forms to refresh your memory as to the specifics of a particular client.

Engagement Letters

Accountants and consultants have all been told to use engagement letters and how important they are in dealing with clients. Engagement letters clarify the scope of the work to be performed, the limitations to the engagement, and the price of the services, among other things. Engagement letters ensure the understanding between the consultant and the client and help prevent miscommunication concerning the engagement.

However, for clients who only need the initial set-up and training, the engagement may be only around four hours. It seems silly to use an engagement letter in those situations and clients sometimes seem surprised when asked to sign an engagement letter. However, if you ever have a dispute with a client, you will wish you had an engagement letter.

"Rather than an engagement letter I use a support agreement which establishes terms without necessarily defining their needs as this is often not accurate because the prospect uses layman's terms. But it sets an hourly price and basic responsibilities. Here in California some clients have problems paying because they do not value or do not understand what technical/troubleshooting services are delivered. So that is why we do not use an engagement letter. Our services are a blend of IT technical and advanced accounting."

ProAdvisors were asked how they use engagement letters in the National ProAdvisor survey and the results are provided in the following chart.

So, you will have to decide when to use engagement letters in your practice. There are several different sample engagement letters for you to download and customize on Intuit's website (accountant.intuit.com).

Session Form

This is a great idea provided in Intuit's Advanced Certification seminar "Expert QuickBooks Consulting: In Pursuit of Service Excellence". The session form is used to document the client meeting, time, items covered during the consulting session, items to be covered next time, and "homework" or "to dos" for the client and consultant. Both the client and consultant should get a copy of the completed form after each session.

It is a great idea to use a session form to document your client engagements. When you get busy and are dealing with numerous clients each week, it is easy to forget the status of each individual client situation. The session forms are a great tool to document the work performed and status of the engagement. You can create your own version of the form or download a generic one and customize it. To download the form, go to accountant.intuit.com, Practice Resources, Seminar Resources, and Seminar Downloads.

Newsletters or Communications with Clients

As a QuickBooks consultant, your client engagements usually are not very long. This is evidenced in the responses provided to the National Survey of ProAdvisors when asked "how many hours is the typical engagement with a client (including follow up sessions)?"

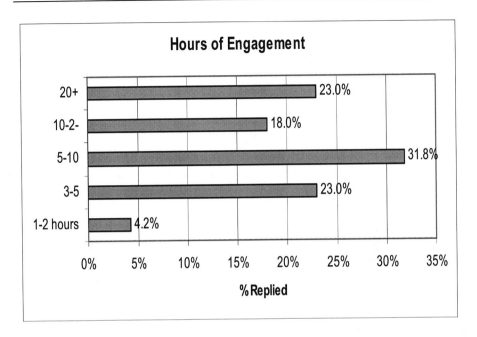

Hours of Engagement

So, you will work with many clients, but each engagement will not be very long. Unless you are able to schedule ongoing support or check-ups with your clients, you typically do not have ongoing contact with the clients. You should try to keep your name in front of your clients so that they do not forget about you and the great service you provided. You also want to encourage them to provide referrals for you!

A monthly or quarterly newsletter is useful to keep in contact with your clients on a regular basis. You can provide short articles related to managing a business, QuickBooks tips and news, or other advice. The important thing is to include your contact information and a reminder that you are available and that referrals are always appreciated. Plus, you can send your newsletters to potential clients or contacts provided they would like to receive your newsletters. You should have them opt in or agree to be on your distribution list, i.e., permission marketing. (Do not forget to include a method for clients to unsubscribe to your newsletters.)

Invoicing and Collection Procedures

As accountants or bookkeepers, you should be on top of your invoicing and collections, but that is not always the case! Sometimes consultants are negligent in tracking time and invoicing promptly. You should develop a method of recording and tracking your time and get in the habit of always writing it down! The session forms discussed earlier will help you track billable time, but you should also keep track of non-billable time and activities.

Depending on the nature of the engagement and the client, you may collect payment at the time of service. This is a great way to train clients on how to write a check in QuickBooks! Then, you can email or send the client a receipt later. This helps improve your cash flow and ensure that you get paid. Do not be afraid or hesitant to ask to be paid! Have you ever had a plumber, HVAC or other service performed where you did not pay at the time of service? Why should your services be any different?

However, if you have a longer engagement or larger client, you may choose to invoice the client. Make sure that you invoice promptly, on a regular basis, and that you include payment terms on the invoice. You should not wait several weeks or a month to invoice clients. Get in the habit of invoicing at least weekly.

You also need to monitor accounts receivable. If a client has not paid you, do not hesitate to send them a reminder invoice with a note to call you if they have any questions or concerns. If the client is dissatisfied for some reason, you need to be aware of it and address the issue. Often, the client is simply busy and overlooked it, and the reminder invoice works.

It is a good idea to have a policy that you do not make appointments with clients who have an outstanding balance. You do not want to keep working for a client without being paid.

Almost every consultant will get burned at least once or twice with a client that does not pay. How aggressively you pursue non-payment is a delicate matter. Sending reminder invoices and/or collection letters is acceptable. You may need to call clients and ask why they have not paid. Usually, clients do not pay because they were dissatisfied with the service or they are having financial difficulties. You should address the issue and negotiate a resolution with the client. Worst case, you may simply have to write it off and learn from the incident.

Chapter 11

Growing the Business

It is hard to get the business started and growing. It takes time to build up your client base, referrals, and a network of contacts. However, once you have built a solid base, the referrals and new clients will come more quickly and your business will start growing quicker. You will experience growing pains so you need to manage the growth properly to ensure your continued success.

Time to Get Help

One of the first issues you are likely to face is that you need help—especially if you started on your own. It makes sense to hire administrative help first. By having someone else take care of administrative tasks (phones, emails, invoicing, filing, bookkeeping, newsletters, and more), you can stay focused on providing good client service, networking to acquire new clients, and increasing your knowledge base.

At some point, you may realize you need another Quick-Books consultant as well. This is where business can become more difficult. You may need someone part time, because you do not have enough work for a full time position. In addition, you want to ensure their knowledge of QuickBooks and their competency—after all, they will be representing you! Make sure you are comfortable with the person's abilities, character, and ethics before you let them represent you to your clients!

If you want to test someone's QuickBooks knowledge, there are some short tests available for your use. Dawn Scranton, (see interview in Appendix D), has created tests called

Employment Guardian for you or your clients to use to test how well someone knows QuickBooks. The Employment Guardian Lite version has ten questions and is available free at www.accountingdirectors.com and the complete version is only $5. Also, there are postings on the community message boards for the ProAdvisors (www.qbadvisor.com) with tests and/or quizzes to use as well.

If you find that you need the help of another QuickBooks consultant, but you do not have enough work to hire someone full time, there are options you can consider. You may consider finding another Certified QuickBooks ProAdvisor to hire as a subcontractor. This could work well especially if you can find someone who does not have much experience and could benefit from working with you.

Other alternatives to finding part-time help includes college students, moms who do not want to work full time but might want to work part time while their kids are in school, retired (or semi-retired) accountants who are not ready to quit working altogether. If you can find someone with the accounting or bookkeeping knowledge already, you should be able to teach them QuickBooks. You could assign them to the easier clients and projects until they build their expertise for the more complex engagements.

If you use sub-contractors, you should have a contract with them that specifies the terms of your agreement with them and includes a confidentiality and non-compete clause as well. You want to protect yourself so that someone cannot steal your clients. Also, keep in mind the difference between employees and sub-contractors and review the "20 question test" at www.irs.gov to make sure you understand the difference. When you hire your first employee (even if he/she is only part time), you must comply with all the payroll withholding and reporting requirements.

Control Growth

You should feel good about your business growing and becoming successful, but you are probably also stressed from too much work and not enough time. You may be tempted to hire someone right away or move into an outside office, but you should make these decisions carefully. You may not actually have enough billable client time to cover the salary of hiring someone full time. It is better to try to find part time help initially. Then, as the billable hours increase, you can increase the hours worked as well. You should do a new cash flow projection before taking on additional overhead expenses.

When you are growing rapidly, it is easy to overlook some details or make careless mistakes. It is important that you maintain good client service and support at all times. You worked hard to build your reputation and you do not want to have dissatisfied clients. If you do make a mistake, acknowledge it promptly and do whatever is possible to fix it and keep the client happy. This may even require an adjustment on a client's billing.

Also, consultants tend to stop networking or marketing when they are busy. Then, when things slow down a bit (and they always will) there is little or no work or new clients. No matter how busy you are, you have to make time for networking and marketing to maintain the contacts and referral network that you worked so hard to develop.

Moving into an Outside Office

If you started your business in a home office, you may consider moving out as the business grows. If you now have employees or sub contractors, you may not want them coming to your home. Maybe you are spending too much time traveling to and from clients and you are tired of meeting in coffee shops.

Maybe you just want to feel like a "real business" by having a "real" office.

Before you make the decision to move out, you should do an informal cost-benefit analysis. Find out what the monthly costs of an outside office will be—rent, utilities, phone, Internet, trash, maintenance, cleaning, snow and ice removal, lawn care, and other expenses you may not have considered (there will always be something unexpected). Make sure that you have sufficient cash flow to cover the increased costs of the office (and employees) during the slow periods as well.

Do not feel like you have to move out to have a "real" office. With technology today, home offices are definitely acceptable! If you really do not want others to know you have a home office, you can always list your office address as 123 Main St., Suite B (where the B can stand for basement or A for Attic) or use a post office box.

Specialization

When starting and growing the business, consultants usually are more of a generalist working with any and all types of clients. When your business has grown, you might take the opportunity to start specializing. If you pick an area to specialize in and can become an "expert" in that area, you can charge higher fees. Dawn Scranton, owner of Accounting Directors, Inc. responded that her income tripled when she decided to specialize in third-party, add-on integration software. (See interview in Appendix D).

When selecting your specialty, there are several things to consider:

► Do you already have more experience in a certain industry—either from clients or prior work experience?

- Which industries do you like working with more?

- Do you have strong IT or technical skills?

- What about the competition—what are the specialties of other ProAdvisors nearby?

- Are there certain types of clients that you want to focus on?

Whatever you decide to specialize in, you should learn everything you can about that industry, type of client, software, etc. If there are trade associations, newsletters, or groups, you should join all of them. You want to become an expert in the area and let everyone know about it! Write articles for the newsletters, conduct seminars, and attending meetings and network.

"FIND the niche you are best at, and market that unique area as much as possible. I did and it increased my business every year."
Nancy M Schiff, "The QuickBooks Guru"
Schiff Management Services,Los Angeles, CA

Retirement Plans and Benefits

During the early years of your business, your profits and cash flow may not allow you to consider retirement plans and benefits. However, once your business has grown, it is time to start considering benefits and ways to minimize your taxes. As an entrepreneur and small business owner, you need to establish your own retirement plan and benefits.

There are several retirement options available to consider:

► SEP – IRA

► Keough

► Roth IRAs

► Solo 401(k)

This is a complex area and the rules vary based on the type of entity you are and whether you have employees. You need to consult with an expert in this area for advice about which option is right for you in your situation. If you do not have any employees now, make sure you ask how hiring employees will affect your plan and whether they are covered under the plan.

Another area you need to research is health insurance (and other insurance as well) for self employed individuals and their families. Many organizations for small businesses may have discounts with certain insurance companies, and there are many insurance companies targeting insurance for small businesses. Again, you need to do some research to determine what is right for you and your business given your situation.

Another thing to note is that as a small business owner you are not required to provide health insurance or retirement benefits to employees. But if you provide it for yourself as the owner, you may need to also provide it for employees. This is a complex matter, so seek professional advice!

Reevaluate the Structure of Business

Now that you have built a successful, profitable business, you may need to reevaluate whether your entity type is still the best for your business. For example, you may have started out as an LLC, but now that you are making so much money you want to consider some tax saving strategies and options. Seek professional advice to reconsider which entity type is now right for you.

Chapter 12

Common Mistakes Consultants Make

We should all learn from our mistakes, and hopefully we can learn from the mistakes of others as well. Not all of these are really mistakes, but they may just give clients or potential clients the wrong impression of your business.

By researching and evaluating other QuickBooks consultants' websites and profiles on the Find-a-ProAdvisors website, you can identify things that probably do not send the right message to potential clients. Also, by talking to clients who have used other ProAdvisors you can learn a lot of good information!

Following are some issues to be aware of as you start and grow your business:

- ► Business cards – It is amazing how many consultants either do not have them or have bad ones! Do NOT print your own business cards—everyone can tell! Besides, by the time you buy the paper for the cards and the ink for the printer, you could have purchased them! Go to www.overnightprints.com or www.vistaprints.com and order some cards now! (See Chapter 8 on Marketing)

- ► Websites – Again, lots of consultants do not have one or it is bad. One consultant had even misspelled Quick-Books on their website!! Also, there are quite a few websites that seem like "used car" type of sales sites. They are crammed full with lots of text and "order here" or "discount" on this or that. They appear desperate to sell you something—anything—just click here! The impression is they are out to "make a buck" any and every way possible. (See Chapter 8 on Marketing)

- ▶ Free email – Some consultants have some reference to QuickBooks in their free email, which is acceptable. Others however, are using free email services like gmail, hotmail, or a number of others. This seems like they are not very serious about their business. (See Chapter 8 on Marketing).

- ▶ Poor (or no) profile on the Find-a-ProAdvisor website – This is free marketing provided by Intuit and can be the source of many referrals. Lots of consultants do not fill out their profile at all or do just the minimum. Put your picture in there and take time to create a good profile. If potential clients like what they see on your profile, they usually call you or go to your website. If they like another consultant's profile better, guess who they are going to call? (See Chapter 9 on Marketing Methods)

- ▶ Not following up on leads or referrals – This is one area that really separates successful people from everyone else. If someone recommends you call so and so, you should make that call! It is much easier to say "John suggested that I give you a call." It is like an introduction and personal referral! You should then also follow up with the person (John) providing the referral and let him know what happened. Successful consulting businesses are built from referrals—you have to follow up on them! (See Chapter 9 on Marketing Methods)

- ▶ Not marketing consistently and continuously – it is tempting to stop attending luncheons or meetings or to stop writing articles, conducting seminars or whatever when you are busy; but you should not do that! You should be marketing and networking constantly—whether you are slow or busy! You need to keep in contact with your network and develop relationships with others to get referrals.

▶ Pricing services too low – Do not fall into the trap of setting low billing rates to get started. It is difficult to later increase your billing rates. Plus, you send the wrong message to potential clients—either that you are cheap and maybe not as good or that you do not value your own expertise. (See Chapter 7 on Define Your Services and Billing Rates)

▶ Accepting a client or job that you are not qualified or ready for – Some consultants have a hard time turning down a potential client. However, if the work is beyond the scope of your expertise or you simply do not have time for that client, you should refer them to another ProAdvisor. If you accept a client that you should not have taken, the chances of the client being dissatisfied with the work, cost, or service is high. When a client is dissatisfied they will tell other people and damage your reputation. (See Chapter 7 on Define Your Services and Billing Rates)

▶ Unprofessional – When you are in business for yourself, you are always representing your business. Be careful how you conduct yourself—even on the weekends at the ball game—you never know when you will see an existing client or meet a potential client! Also, always keep in mind that anything you post on the web might be seen by a client.

▶ Not carrying around Simple Start – You should carry Simple Start with you wherever you go! When you meet someone and they tell you they have just started a business, you can hand them a copy of Simple Start and tell them you are there for them if the need help. Order stickers with your contact information to place on Simple Start or make sure you give them your business card! It is a great marketing tool and Intuit provides Simple Start for free!

Chapter 13

Advice from Other ProAdvisors

The following are the responses from the National Survey of ProAdvisors to the following question: **What advice do you have for other/new QB consultants?**

- ► Persistence Pays Off!

- ► QuickBooks clients can lead to tax prep work if you offer that service and visa-versa

- ► Stay flexible, listen to your customers and keep your skill level sharp!!

- ► Require a credit card # for all engagements

- ► Keep it simple, KNOW your QuickBooks inside and out

- ► Develop and use a business plan to help you stay on track.

- ► Marketing is key!

- ► Don't be a consultant on all software out there, dedicate to it so you can really provide quality services. If you are in over your head, admit it and get help.

- ► Start networking with other professionals early. Swap services in the beginning with some of your vendors - local advertising publications are good.

- ► Get a signed contract or get payment/partial payment upfront.

- ► LEARN the software; put your own business on Quick-Books; use online banking; kick the tires!

- ► Challenge clients to think "beyond bookkeeping"

- ► Try to solve your clients pain points rather than just teach them how to use QuickBooks. Make yourself their go-to person when they have questions, they call you.
  Dawn Ashpole
  SBA Services, Inc.
  Portland, OR

- ► Provide good customer service and your clients will pass your name on to other prospective clients.

- ► Don't under price yourself.

- ► Specialize where you are qualified, Get help or don't take engagements for which you are not qualified.

- ► Listen to your clients long enough to provide solutions that accomplish the whole picture.
  Anna Sheets, Accounting Made Simple, Valparaiso, IN

- ► Try to build relationships with multiple accounting firms. Get Certified in every possible product and be sure to do it every year.

- ► Attend trainings & conferences (even if they are a distance or costly), it is an investment in your business. You will meet other ProAdvisors who will give you great ideas about building your business. Read Everything you can get your hands on.
  Carolyn A. Dauphin, ACQA, Lindenhurst, NY
  www.CDMobileService.com

▶ Go for the Certifications in QuickBooks as much as you can. Learn about everything related to QuickBooks, third party software, and payroll, which kinds of software to buy and take the test every year. Try to hook up with CPA's. They are a good source of referrals. Get your name out there.
Susan Rosenberg, Roslyn, NY

▶ It's all about meeting people....networking.

▶ Update your Advisor status every year as quickly as possible & get certified in POS and Enterprise Solution.

▶ Use QuickBooks yourself. Setup A/P, A/R, play with different invoices, loading Logo's, etc. Learn how to setup payroll and sales tax items, as these will be one of the first questions a new client will ask you.
Scott Fullerton CPA, Blue Springs, MO

▶ Pick your clients carefully and you will avoid headaches down the road!
Dan Mc Gonagle, Los Angeles

▶ Don't try and be an "expert" after passing one or 2 years of certification. I have redone so many set ups and retained offices from "Newbies" QuickBooks Advisors. I am doing one now that someone thought she was upgrading a client—a VERY large client. Took 4 months and it's still wrong. I have been called in to "fix" it. This Advisor could have avoided this 3 months ago, called for help and still come out looking fine. As it is, her "credentials" speak for themselves

▶ Be Flexible. There is always more than one solution for the same problem. Listen to your client. Get involved in the community.

▶ Learn as much as possible about the program; there are so many free and inexpensive ways to do this. You will be loved by your clients if you have a ready answer.

▶ Be honest with your clients if you don't know something.

▶ Learn the program, and don't be afraid to try things - but always back up first.

▶ Don't assume the client knows anything. Be gracious and say "perhaps you already know this, but…

▶ Sometimes the smallest detail makes a huge difference.

▶ Be prepared to receive data from clients who do not have computers in various formats. Try to set up simple record keeping forms for those clients and be prepared to teach business owners bookkeeping and how important it is to their business.

▶ I would suggest spending time training yourself on additional QuickBooks, tips & tricks and certifications. Never stop. Knowledge is Power! Billable Power!
Michael Peters, Abacus Rex, Lombard Illinois

▶ Specialize in a specific industry, business-type

▶ Have a good plan to hire and train employees, you CAN'T do it all by yourself!

▶ Get to know QuickBooks well. Get to know some of the adds ons that your clients can use.

► Learn the product really well. Don't get down on yourself if you don't know the answer. You can't possibly know the answer to every question a client can have. Get to know other advisors and join as many groups that have other advisors as you can. This way when you don't know the answer you can find someone who does. Don't ever negotiate on price. Clients who want to nickel and dime you are on the wrong side of the 80/20 rule. They will complain the most, suck up a ton of time and then not pay you.
Terri Wilson, Offcierge Inc., Cincinnati, OH

► Learn the program and it's capabilities

► Rather than an engagement letter I use a support agreement which establishes terms without necessarily defining their needs as this is often not accurate because the prospect uses layman's terms. But it sets an hourly price and basic responsibilities. Here in California some clients have problems paying because they do not value or do not understand what technical/troubleshooting services are delivered. So that is why we do not use an engagement letter. Our services are a blend of IT technical and advanced accounting.

► Be familiar with Balance Sheet, Income Statements and correctly applying charges to the right expense accounts.

► Make sure you know what your market place will tolerate when you set your fees, do your research. Be honest with your clients; don't promise something you can't deliver. I've heard over and over, previous people the client hired didn't know what they were doing.

► Don't let your training stop at the certification test. There are many training options available to you.
Sandy Robertson, Tampa FL

► In the QuickBooks Accountant Update seminar last November 2006, they stated that QuickBooks consultants should get as much information as possible before a visit. (and provided information of suggested questions to ask.) Pay attention to that process because the more you know of the client the more prepared you will appear to the client, which can secure an on-going client/relationship.

► Also, some clients want to be your "friend", which will only open a door to freebies outside your original agreements. Be friendly and maintain a professional business relationship. See this coming before it happens. Sometimes it can break a contract because what they want of you is something that will take time and not want to pay the extras, they want a throw-in.

► You shouldn't just use the QuickBooks Advisor program to just get referrals. You need to know your stuff to be successful and to not make it a nightmare for your client.

► I learned from someone else's advice and maybe someone can learn by my adding this to our "advice column". Try to differentiate yourself from others. For example, your first hour of QuickBooks consulting for a new client can be free. Also, always remember to inform your prospective new client of your ProAdvisor discount on ordering software and supplies.
Mary P. Harris, Harris Accounting and Bookkeeping
Bel Air, MD

► Charge a lot. Don't work cheap.

► Get the Sleeter reference guide. Their training is superior!

- ► I started by working as a subcontractor to an accounting firm that offered QuickBooks training and support to its clients. Over time I developed my own clients, but still provide services to accounting firms who prefer to out-source this service than staff internally.

- ► Don't underestimate your abilities, and don't under price your services. Consider travel time to and from clients, and consider research time and price accordingly. Remember, YOU are the EXPERT!

- ► You must love people, Quickbooks, and business. A QuickBooks consultant needs to be proficient in all three.

- ► Become a proadvisor

- ► Continuing education

- ► Join Sleeter Group

- ► Don't under value your services.

- ► Be sure you take the test and become a Pro-Advisor each year. The benefits far outweigh the cost and time. Consider joining the Sleeter Group. There is a lot of valuable information and resources. The conference is excellent.

- ► Take & pass the proadvisor exam each year

- ► Find a niche. Since it is difficult to be an expert in all industries, pick one or two and excel in it.

▶ Know your Accounting better than you know QuickBooks. Be flexible with applying your QuickBooks and accounting knowledge with clients. Talk about their business and how they like to do things, if they need the detail of job costing or are fine with just showing income and expense. Try to put yourself in their place and keep it as simple as possible. Introduce more complex methods to those that can handle it, but always step back when you feel they are getting overwhelmed. There is no such thing as the "correct" way to use QuickBooks, customize the process to what works for them, or they won't want to use QuickBooks.
Karen Cook, Wayne A Blosberg, PA, Coon Rapids, MN.

▶ It is essential that you immerse your self in as much Quickbooks information as you can get your hands on. You never know when a client well have specific problem that you have heard about. Join the forums and absorb as much as you can.

▶ Ask enough questions of a potential client in the initial interview to be sure QuickBooks is the correct accounting solution for their needs.

▶ Pick an industry to specialize in

▶ Make sure you know the software and the quirks that go along with it, especially if you are switching software.

▶ I have found that advertising in the local paper has been a waste of money. Other CPA's in the area have told me the same. Getting your business is best through referrals and it takes time.

▶ Get certified and get your advanced certification.
Rebecca Brown, NGAC, Inc., Canton, GA

▶ Pick out a specialty (bookkeeping vs. tax).

- Join networking groups like Biznik, Le Tip, BNI, WEN, etc.

- Don't be afraid to walk door to door to ask for business.

- Advertise your services in detail on Craig's List and include a photo.

- Fill out your QuickBooks ProAdvisor profile completely. Keith Gormezano, A Better Temporary, Inc., Seattle, WA

- Attend as many seminars and classes as possible. As someone who does not actually use the product on a daily basis, there are a lot of features that you clients will want to use that you may not be familiar with. Learn from your clients. Ask them how they use the different features of the product and any shortcuts etc that they use.

- Use the support services that are available through QuickBooks ProAdvisor Program. You have a strong and well tested knowledge base to draw from, use it.

- Never never call yourself a QuickBooks Consultant UNLESS you know the software inside out. Learning the QuickBooks software thoroughly is your very first step.

- Keep in mind that QuickBooks for Mac is a very different product and do not offer your services for Mac users without experience!

- Find an accountant to partner with

- Know accounting and network, network, network

- Be diligent. Do what you say you're going to do, when you say you're going to do it. Your good name is worth much.

- Get certified and work with the product in and out

▶ Clearly understand the current business issue and the impact the solution will have going forward as well as the intended use of the QuickBooks data element and application. QuickBooks has a great functionality do not jury rig them.

▶ You must know accounting and you need to know QuickBooks very well

▶ Take courses in bookkeeping to gain some knowledge in this area

▶ Use QuickBooks personally, so you really know it.

▶ You can't know everything, so don't pretend that you do. But you will impress clients by knowing where to get the answers, and getting back to them quickly.

▶ If you are a QuickBooks Consultant and not an accountant, the best way to grow your client base is to partner with accounting, legal and financial professionals where both parties can refer business to the other.
Vincent F. Triolo, Small Biz Assist, Allentown, PA

▶ Do not work cheaply!

▶ Do not under price your services, it takes time to get new business, therefore understand and communicate the benefits of your services to the client.

▶ This first thing you must do is complete your website set up. I get most of my referrals from the Quickbooks website.   Brad Lee White Sr., BW Consulting., Brooklyn, NY

▶ Don't "wing it". Be a professional. Be well-trained. In a sense, one of us can represent all of us. Realize the client is paying for expertise--make sure they get it!
Debbi C. Warden, CPA, MBA, The Business Manager, LLC, Centennial, CO

▶ Be honest; admit it when you don't know something or when you make a mistake. Always follow through on returning phone calls, providing support and doing what you said you would do, even if you can't always charge for it. It usually always pays off.
Paulette Dreher, SBS Associates, Inc., Westwood, NJ

▶ Use QuickBooks as much as possible.

▶ Encourage QBOE (QuickBooks Online Edition) so that you have quicker access client's account.

▶ They should learn the program thoroughly and learn all that it can do and advise and teach clients the excellent reporting it has. Fred Shetka, Tom Lewis Associates PA, St Paul, MN

▶ Learn the product inside and out

▶ Focus on just a few areas of expertise. And become the best at those.

▶ With regard to training clients, start with basic features that they will use (setting up vendor and customer database; entering & paying bills; entering customer invoices & receiving payments; running Balance Sheet & Profit & Loss Reports; payroll; bank reconciliation). After they understand these features, then move on to the more complex (job costing, etc.)

▶ Know your bookkeeping (full charge)/accounting skills before advising others. Knowing how bookkeeping is done manually helps. How journals are posted to ledgers and how the ledger accounts should look.

▶ Estimate high, you always run into more problems than you expect

▶ Get paid at time of service. Use engagement letters. When I train new users, I have THEM sit at the computer to do the work, rather than me doing it and showing them. I also have made up QuickBooks "cheat sheets" that I give to new clients - how to do common tasks - so they have something to refer to later.

▶ The QuickBooks ProAdvisor program and my listing on their website has helped me to grow my business more than any other advertising campaign. Thank you Intuit!

▶ Get in there, roll up your sleeves, and play with that software! That and the QuickBooks Certification Exams / QuickBooks provided training will do the trick!
Gregory J. Randazzo, CPA, Midwest Accounting, P.C., Clinton Twp., MI 48038, www.mwaccounting.com

▶ Aggressive marketing is required

▶ If you are not the best of the best ... focus on bookkeeping and tax prep business

▶ Take advantage of all of the information QuickBooks offers its consultants. It is one of the most proactive marketing companies for its ProAdvisors.
Marc Adams, MCA Certified Tax Preparers, Teaneck, NJ

▶ Get certified! It is a no brainer.

Chapter 14

What Consultants Wish They Had Known Sooner

The following are the responses from the National Survey of ProAdvisors to the following question: **What do you wish you would have known sooner or done differently in your business?**

- ▶ To constantly be marketing my business...even during the very busy times.

- ▶ I would have trained my staff at every level more thoroughly in the software. Depth of knowledge can be invaluable.

- ▶ Pushed QuickBooks's services

- ▶ I wish I used prepaid blocks of time earlier.

- ▶ Create Relationships with Developers, Develop Negotiation Skills, Develop mid-market "Systems" Knowledge

- ▶ I wish I had fully understood about Intuit and their policies for ProAdvisors and the referral database.

- ▶ After 19 yrs I still enjoy getting up and going to work everyday. I can't think of anything I'd do differently.
  Dawn Ashpole, SBA Services, Inc., Portland, OR

- ▶ IT is important

- Not getting a signed contract or engagement letter before starting a project. Not getting a retainer to start large projects. Every project now (large or small) has a contract & retainer.

- Nothing everything worked out perfect. Go for the certifications in QuickBooks as much as you can.

- How much to charge-know what others are charging in the area

- Started my own business earlier! Also, I felt I needed to take on every client that came in the door. I paid for that with no pays, slow pays, trade labor and write-offs that all were in the way of the good clients.
  Scott Fullerton CPA, Blue Springs, MO

- I wish I would have gotten certified sooner.

- To charge more for my services - I am a great resource for my clients.

- Pricing

- Direct advertising program

- Not waiver in my price I charge to clients.

- Become a QB certified Pro Advisor

- Established a firm policy of pricing and collection for services performed.

► First and foremost spend as many business hours meeting with business people talking about your business. The local Chamber Of Commerce is a great place to meet other business owners.

   Helpful Hint: When you are networking with Chamber members work hard to get them business before your ask. People are more willing to help if you show you help them first

► The back office work can be done anytime day or night.

► Less dependence on Intuit for advertising exposure and more on myself

► Used Engagement letters better, they help so much with client expectations and getting paid.

► Focus more and sooner on QuickBooks

► Maybe...not to try to do so much right away. I think I've tried to do too much in my first year. I marketed bookkeeping, payroll, training, support, all aspects of QB consulting, as well as 3rd party integration. I am now pulling back and decreasing my focus. I will widen my focus more slowly as I grow and can afford support staff.

► Payroll Familiarity with a focus on timing of Payroll liabilities to the various taxing agencies.

► Concentrated on Implementation, Training and Support at the start of my business.

► More marketing.

► So far, everything is going well.

► I wish I could have found out more concrete info on how other consultants grow and run their businesses

▶ Use engagement letters and ask for retainers. Look at their unpaid bills report. If they don't pay other people, they won't pay you. Do a file analysis before you touch anything.

▶ Nothing, In 4 years the business has grown steadily

▶ I started thinking that I would provide training as my core revenue stream. However, I quickly realized that for each client trained, I was working myself out of a job. So I had to start developing on-going accounting clients.

▶ I wish I'd found the page that tells what the average rates other Advisors are charging.

▶ Pricing....I gave "deals" to my customers when I first started, and am still trying to get my rates up to something more realistic with them.

▶ I wish I had started my own business earlier.

▶ Attend the free update seminars by Intuit each year when the new version is released. Free software has been provided in the past. Pay strict attention to the user license. It is a one person license, unless otherwise purchased.

▶ Went out on my own

▶ charged more per hour and reject "iffy" clients

▶ I probably would have attended more training sessions before I hung my shingle.

▶ That's difficult to answer, since every day is a learning process. There is always the "if I had known this then, I would have done it differently back then" aspect.

▶ How beneficial it is to be a Certified in Quickbooks.

- That QuickBooks, while a great small business accounting software, is not an out of the box solution for many clients. Especially, if they do not have any accounting training.

- Keep up with the newsletter and website info more often

- Be willing to say NO to potential clients who don't fit my areas of interest or expertise. Make contact with other Advisors, so I can refer them to someone more appropriate.

- Become a CPA

- I wish I had known of the QuickBooks ProAdvisor Program and joined it when I first started. It is too bad that they don't have a first year rate or only provide the services but not the software for a discounted rate. Keith Gormezano, A Better Temporary, Inc., Seattle, WA

- I wish I would have taken the approach of being a consultant sooner and not a "bookkeeper" who knew how to use QuickBooks.

- There will be times that you are better served by referring a client to another pro advisor

- I would have hired employees instead of taking on partners when I needed help.

- Engagement letters for every engagement

- Gotten more hands-on experience before certification.

- Learned how to use QODBC

- Billing rate range for various services in the area

▶ Insisting that every QuickBooks client stay current with the latest version. If they can't afford to buy the next release, then they can't afford me either.

▶ The need for competent QuickBooks consulting is much higher than initially assumed.

▶ Time management and more competitive pricing of services.

▶ The going rate for consulting services. I was never sure if I was charging enough.

▶ I didn't charge enough for a long time. It took me a while to catch up because I couldn't reasonably increase my hourly rate to existing clients by large sums! Also, I think I was (still can be) overly generous with my time.
Debbi C. Warden, CPA, MBA, The Business Manager, LLC, Centennial, CO

▶ We wasted a lot of time and money on Brochures, Advertising and Networking that generally speaking did not pay off. However, you have to start somewhere, until referrals start coming in.
Paulette Dreher, SBS Associates, Inc., Westwood, NJ

▶ Would have gone into business for myself sooner.

▶ QBOE (QuickBooks Online Edition)

▶ Started using QuickBooks sooner as it is easy to teach to clients that start it from the beginning.

▶ How to get rid of bad clients

▶ How to turn down bad clients. Just say no to certain projects. Stay clear of dishonest or dysfunctional clients.

▶ How to chargeing. Value billing.

- ▶ Standardize instead of customize

- ▶ When starting my first practice, I used my home address which happened to be in an upscale area familiar to most people. When starting my second practice from a less well-known part of town, I should have had an office or virtual office two years before I did. Working from your home address (unless it's in an affluent/upscale/well-known neighborhood) often leads to calls from only other home-based businesses in the same area.

- ▶ I didn't charge a high enough rate in the beginning. I now charge travel time to clients who are more than 10 miles away or so. I also now have a 2-hour minimum. This year, I plan to require my older clients to upgrade to newer versions of QuickBooks at least every two or three years -I'm still supporting people who have QuickBooks 3.0!! But not for much longer...

- ▶ Get paid in advance

- ▶ Think strategies, strategic alliances, partnerships, and synergies. 1 + 1 = 3.
  Gregory J. Randazzo, CPA, Midwest Accounting, P.C.
  Clinton Twp., MI, www.mwaccounting.com

- ▶ Worked for another consultant before i started my own business.

- ▶ Smaller accounts are not worth the time and effort expended

- ▶ I wish that I would have known how much education the Certified ProAdvisor guides (webinars and materials) offer. I thought because you can become a ProAdvisor simply for paying the QuickBooks fee that it was a gimmick. In a lot of ways it is, but the Certification is so much more than what I would have expected.

Chapter 15

Keys to Success

The following are the responses from the National Survey of ProAdvisors to the following question: **What would you say are the keys to building a successful QuickBooks consulting business?**

- ► Knowledge of the subject matter (accounting, technology)

- ► Right type of promotion, exposure (not necessarily advertising)

- ► A good business plan.

- ► Always be selling.

- ► Providing excellent service to your clients.

- ► Know your stuff.

- ► Know the software inside and out. Make money, watch the clock, but help your clients succeed and they will remember you and refer you business.

- ► Be willing to network.

- ► Getting the word out.

- ► Doing a good job; providing value to your clients; referrals!!!

- ► Be knowledgeable, efficient and open minded.

- ► Don't get buried in paperwork - that's what data-entry people are for.... focus on profitable relationships

- I wouldn't consider mine successful yet...

- Treat it like a 9-5 job. You can't know or do everything so know where to find the support you need and be very very good at what you do know.
  Dawn Ashpole, SBA Services, Inc., Portland, OR

- Keeping up with the certifications so your name is always visible.

- Flexibility with your clients and providing customized services for each of them

- Be available, don't give away your services.

- Building Trust in client relationships and providing value to their business.

- Following this motto: "Say what you mean, and mean what you say". Always be a straight shooter with your clients.

- Always do the "right" thing for the client.

  Carolyn A. Dauphin, ACQA, Custom Integrated Accounting Solutions, NY, www.CDMobileService.com

- Know your materials and more. you need to be able to be an educated consultant and give clients all the options. Third party software, payroll, the different kinds of QuickBooks software to buy, gotomypc, remote access. Etc

- Hard to say, as I wouldn't consider my QuickBooks consulting a large, successful part of my overall business yet.

- Constant contact & quick follow-up with clients

- Networking. Let people know you specialize in Quick-Books. Scott Fullerton CPA, Blue Springs, MO

- Finding the right marketing approach!

- FIND the niche you are best at, and market that unique area as much as possible. I did and it increased my business every year
  Nancy M Schiff, "The QuickBooks Guru"
  Schiff Management Services, Los Angeles, CA

- Listening to your clients needs.

- Getting to know tax practitioners who do not want to learn QuickBooks - they want to concentrate on tax work and are happy to find me.

- Referrals

- Proper training and good follow up.

- Do taxes and bookkeeping too. They are natural fits with QuickBooks consulting and provide a lot of referral business.

- Be consistent. Do what you say you're going to do. Be honest about your limitations.

- Be sincere with each client, honest, helpful, provide timely, accurate service and above all do not make your client feel inferior.

- Sales-If you don't think you can sell. Learn the basics or find a partner. No Sales --No Business

- Knowledge , Knowledge, Knowledge

- ▶ Solution Selling: You aren't selling a Product. You are selling yourself first and then you are a problem solver. Michael Peters, Abacus Rex, Lombard Illinois

- ▶ Quality Employees

- ▶ Quality Customer Service

- ▶ Personable

- ▶ Know clients' requirements

- ▶ A good accounting and IT background since you need to be able to set up QuickBooks, solve QuickBooks problems and also solve computer issues that effect QuickBooks. You need to build good relationships with your clients.

- ▶ Focus on just a few industries and start there. Really get to know these industries and how to setup and use QuickBooks within that industry. Create and always use good engagement letters. Create a good time management routine. Take time to work on your business every week...reviewing and revising business plan, goals, etc.

- ▶ Understanding the clients needs and experience

- ▶ Learn managerial accounting - too many CPAs only care about tax accounting. So it is easy to differentiate from their services.

- ▶ have real world business experience

- ▶ Knowledge, Dedication, Perseverance and a good advertising strategy.

- Be honest with your clients, don't promise them services you can't deliver, follow up, taking every class you can get your hands on to learn QB, and use QB for your own business. Read the material Intuit sends, it's wonderful.

- Know the product, accounting and your client's business.

- QuickBooks referral database!!!

- Expert knowledge of the programs.

- Be proactive.

- Knowing the product thoroughly.

- My enjoyment of teaching comes across to the customers. Also my prior business experience is actual and practical something accountants do not have.

- Certification training and credentials, and developing a good relationship with your clients. Don't be afraid to cold call businesses and accounting firms to market your services.

- Never turn down a client, give out only enough "free" information to let a potential client know that you know what you are talking about, and ask satisfied clients to advertise for you by passing out your business cards.

- Referrals are the cornerstone of my business. Also patience...if a prospective client doesn't go with you at first, they eventually will. If a client uses you, chances are you'll get another call a few months down the road.

- I built my practice doing local seminars. Tripled the year I did this. This is very time consuming, but you can break even. I suggest the Sleeter materials and their "Train the Trainer" seminar.

- ▶ Networking, doing the job right

- ▶ Experience and training.

- ▶ Contacts and referrals

- ▶ Quality, professionalism, good ethics

- ▶ The keys to building a successful QuickBooks consulting business are specifically to 'listen' to what the client wants to accomplish and make recommendations in order for the client to accomplish these goals.

- ▶ A successful QuickBooks consultant must have a strong accounting background in order to apply the QuickBooks processes that are best suited to a particular client and industry. QuickBooks consulting is far more than training someone on the functions of QuickBooks - the Help file and books can do that. You have to train a client how to use QuickBooks in a manner that leads to producing accurate financial information and introduce them to the capabilities of financial decision-making based on the reliable financial data from QuickBooks. Once you learn to provide a well-rounded service to your clients, the referrals will come. Karen Cook, Wayne A Blosberg, PA, Coon Rapids, MN.

- ▶ Customer service and knowing what your clients want inside and out.

- ▶ Explaining to potential clients that they will need to allocate time to learn the software.

- ▶ Networking and building alliances within the local chamber or other local group and specializing in a specific industry such as retailing, auto

- Be consistent. Be clear. Communicate what you will do, and follow through in a timely manner. Create realistic expectations.

- Get involved in your community. I joined the local Chamber of Commerce and although I have only received 2 clients through the Chamber, I have been able to make many contacts. Currently, I serve as the Treasurer for the Chamber.

- Always answer e-mails promptly. Be there for them

- Let everyone know you are in business and work 60 hours a week. Keith Gormezano, A Better Temporary, Inc., Seattle, WA

- Training on a regular basis, not just when renewing your ProAdvisor status. Develop structure in your company so that all consulting services adhere to a best practices strategy. This will start a very positive and steady "buzz" on the street for your firm and bring you referrals.

- The key to building a successful QuickBooks consulting business is to provide excellent service. You will develop a great reputation and then referrals will kick in.

- Follow up with previous clients

- Experience, experience, experience

- Being organized

- Be dependable. Never make your clients feel stupid or inferior. Don't burn bridges.

- Sell add-on products, keep the client buying services from you, whether quarterly reviews, or IT services or checks and forms

▶ Creatively and business experience on how to implement software applications.

▶ Hands on experience, certification, networking, advertising.

▶ Know what you are talking about and provide excellent customer service

▶ References

▶ Be willing to be helpful, even if for free for quick questions or to begin setup of a new client.

▶ Find out what the client needs in the first meeting, then decide whether or not you can help them. If you can't, refer them to an associate.

▶ Network with other business professionals.

▶ Provide high quality services for which you are qualified, and do not undercharge for your services. Do not compete based on price. Use non-price competition.

▶ Building relationships with clients and referral base like CPAs.

▶ Referrals from prior happy customers

▶ Keep your website updated, people really look at it, no matter how many consultants they see, you never know what a client is looking for, they could be looking for you.

▶ Good communication w/client regarding estimated time and fees and results.

▶ Certification, certification, certification

▶ Honesty with Clients

▶ Without a doubt, a combination of education and experience--you HAVE to know the accounting for the decisions you make as you record and you have to know the accounting of what QuickBooks is doing (that you might not see). The experience in both industry and with QuickBooks makes you worthy of charging a fee for your services. The accounting experience helps you guide your clients and customize client reports-- and the QuickBooks experience helps you set up & problem solve within the software in a professionally effective manner. There is always more to learn.
Debbi C. Warden, CPA, MBA
The Business Manager, LLC, Centennial, CO

▶ Experience, honesty and perhaps most importantly creative thinking, as every client is different even when there are many similarities.
Paulette Dreher, SBS Associates, Inc., Westwood, NJ

▶ Learn. Learn. Learn. Teach.

▶ Staying in contact with the clients. Making sure they understand how QuickBooks works and how to properly record all transactions so that at year end we have no messes to have to clean up.

▶ Building trusting relationships. Treat each client as if they were your only client.

▶ Being accessible and responsive to client's needs in a timely fashion; being able to answer client's questions so they can understand; training clients so they can use QB to its fullest.

▶ Having a strong bookkeeping (full charge), accounting and tax background, computer savvy

▶ Knowledge, contacts

- Effective marketing and business development.

- Strong technical competence.

- Client service/relationship with client.

- Stay on top of latest technology; good teaching skills; good listening skills

- Become Certified. Listen to Clients needs

- I don't charge for 10 minute QuickBooks phone calls and I tell client this upfront. I also use (and provide to my clients free of charge) the Remote Accounting Service (RAS) to transfer QuickBooks files back and forth - I feel this is one of the keys to a successful QuickBooks consulting practice, and it makes my life so much easier! I use their "Netviewer" program and am able to access the client's desktop from my office to trouble-shoot.

- Training, knowledge, experience and good customer service skills plus a listing on the QuickBooks ProAdvisor website.

- You better be affordable to start. Sprinkle yourself (the high priced consultant) into the mix of less experienced QuickBooks Advisors / bookkeepers, get the client to help him or herself, and provide a power assist! Gregory J. Randazzo, CPA, Midwest Accounting, P.C. Clinton Twp., MI, www.mwaccounting.com

- Professionalism & aggressive marketing.

- That you identify what makes you unique and focus on that

Appendix A

National ProAdvisor Survey Results

In August, 2007 a survey was emailed to approximately 800 ProAdvisors from cities across the United States and a link to the survey was posted on QuickBooks ProAdvisor community message boards. A total of 267 ProAdvisors responded and completed the survey. The survey was not scientific and the answers provided were not verified for validity. There is no assurance that the answers provided are complete or honest

1. Which of the following describes you? (mark all that apply

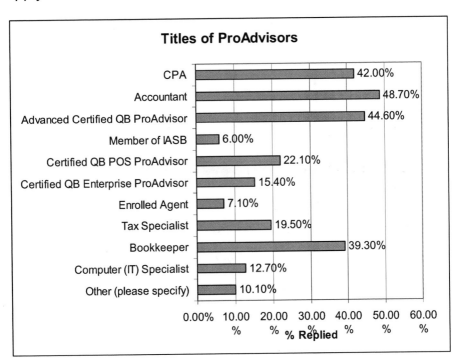

Titles of ProAdvisors

Title	% Replied
CPA	42.00%
Accountant	48.70%
Advanced Certified QB ProAdvisor	44.60%
Member of IASB	6.00%
Certified QB POS ProAdvisor	22.10%
Certified QB Enterprise ProAdvisor	15.40%
Enrolled Agent	7.10%
Tax Specialist	19.50%
Bookkeeper	39.30%
Computer (IT) Specialist	12.70%
Other (please specify)	10.10%

2. As to providing QuickBooks services, which best describes your current situation?

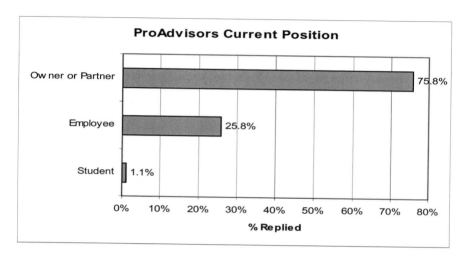

3. If you are an employee or student, how likely are you to start your own accounting, bookkeeping, tax preparation or consulting business?

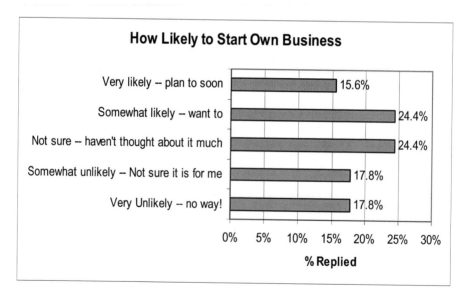

4. How do you use an engagement letter:

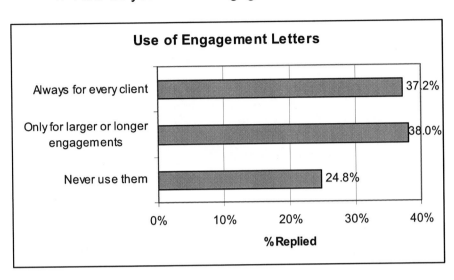

5. How many employees (full time equivalent) or subcontractors do you have?

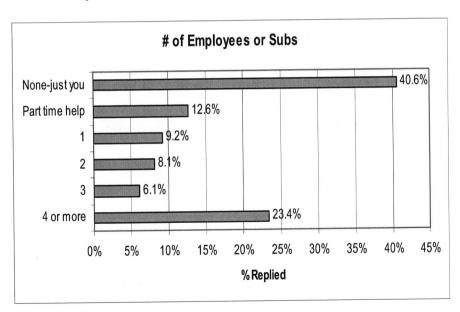

6. How much is your annual gross income from Quick-Books related consulting?

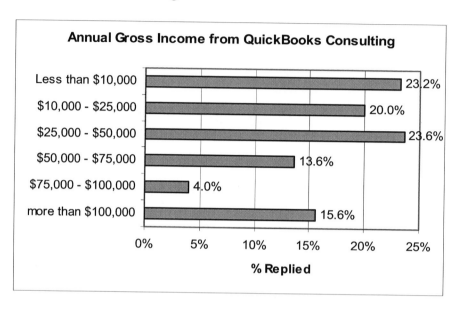

7. How many years have you been providing Quick-Books consulting services?

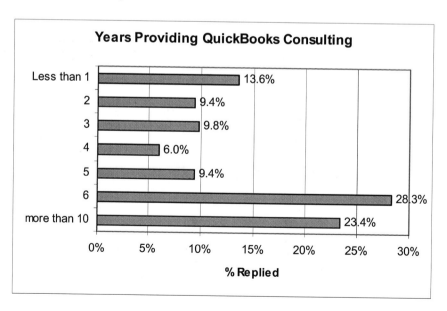

8. How much of your business is QuickBooks related services? (vs. tax, bookkeeping, or other)

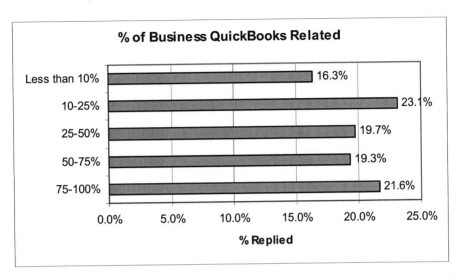

% of Business QuickBooks Related

	% Replied
Less than 10%	16.3%
10-25%	23.1%
25-50%	19.7%
50-75%	19.3%
75-100%	21.6%

9. What other services do you provide? (mark all that apply)

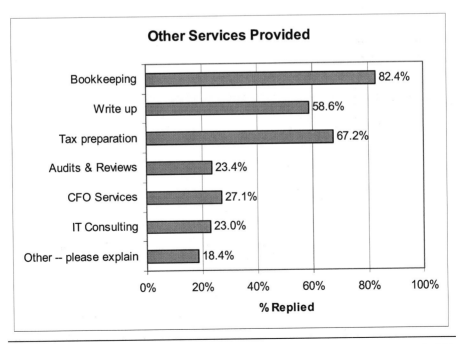

Other Services Provided

	% Replied
Bookkeeping	82.4%
Write up	58.6%
Tax preparation	67.2%
Audits & Reviews	23.4%
CFO Services	27.1%
IT Consulting	23.0%
Other -- please explain	18.4%

10. What size of clients have you worked with based on number of employees? (mark all that apply)

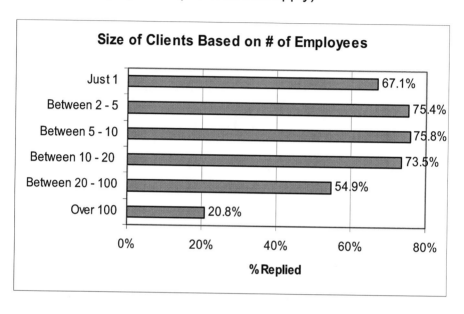

11. How many hours is the typical engagement with a client? (including follow-up sessions)

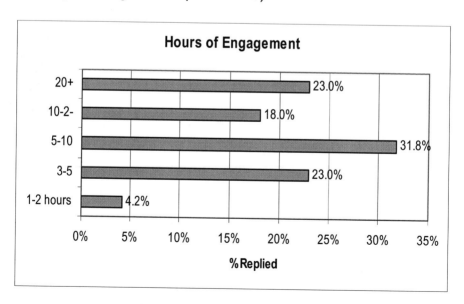

12. What type of marketing do you use for your business (mark all that apply) and how would you rate its effectiveness?

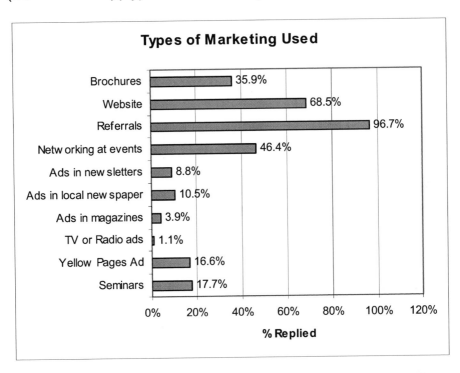

	Very Effec- tive	Some- what Effective	Somewhat Ineffective	Very Ineffec- tive
Brochures	6.5%	50.6%	28.6%	14.3%
Website	26.2%	47.5%	18.9%	7.4%
Referrals	79.8%	16.7%	2.4%	1.2%
Networking	22.1%	53.7%	18.9%	5.3%
Ads in newsletters	3.7%	18.5%	44.4%	33.3%
Ads in local news- paper	0.0%	21.9%	37.5%	40.6%
Ads in magazines	0.0%	16.7%	38.9%	44.4%
TV or Radio ads	0.0%	23.1%	38.5%	38.5%
Yellow Pages ad	7.0%	51.2%	14.0%	27.9%
Seminars	43.9%	31.7%	22.0%	2.4%

13. Do you specialize in any of the following industries? (mark all that apply)

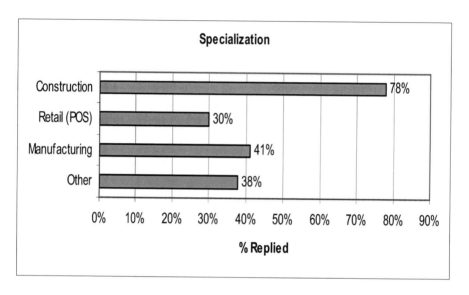

Appendix B

Intuit 2007 Rates Survey

The 2007 Rates Survey from Intuit ProConnection newsletter provides a wealth of useful information about billing rates. Bill Teague, managing editor of the newsletter, wrote several excellent articles discussing the survey, methodology, and analyzing the results in depth. This is the link to the articles: http://accountant.intuit.com/practice_resources/articles/practice_development/index.aspx. The following pages are a few key tables excerpted from the articles.

Hourly Rates Overview Table

Response	General Book-keeping	Non-Software Business Consulting	Generating Reports	Software Install/ Setup	Troubleshooting	Training	On-site Mainte-nance	Telephone Consulting
Count	750	701	670	666	662	652	601	524
Average	$61	$95	$73	$86	$82	$81	$81	$79
Low	$10	$15	$10	$15	$15	$15	$15	$10
High	$180	$350	$300	$1000	$300	$350	$350	$265
Mode (Most Frequent)	$50	$75	$75	$75	$75	$75	$75	$75

Fixed Fees Overview Table

Response	Installation and Setup (New User)	Quarterly Tune-Up	Personal Training (1-2 Hrs.)	Personal Training (3-4 Hrs.)	Personal Training (Full Day)
Count	323	311	280	276	257
Average	321	246	153	287	565
Low	25	25	25	25	50
High	3000	1200	540	600	1500
Mode	250	150	150	200	500

Bookkeepers (No ProAdvisors or CPAs)
Hourly Rates Overview

Response	General Book-keeping	Non-Software Business Consulting	Generating Reports	Software Install/ Setup	Troubleshooting	Training	On-site Mainte-nance	Telephone Consulting
Count	223	195	205	203	198	207	185	151
Average	**$48**	**$65**	**$53**	**$65**	**$59**	**$61**	**$59**	**$52**
Low	$10	$15	$15	$15	$15	$15	$15	$10
High	$100	$250	$250	$250	$165	$150	$165	$150
Mode (Most Frequent)	$50	$50	$50	$75	$75	$75	$75	$50

Fixed Fees Overview

Response	Installation and Setup (New User)	Quarterly Tune-Up	Personal Training (1-2 Hrs.)	Personal Training (3-4 Hrs.)	Personal Training (Full Day)
Count	92	83	88	85	78
Average	**$243**	**$206**	**$124**	**$239**	**$483**
Low	$25	$25	$25	$50	$75
High	$1500	$1000	$300	$525	$1000
Mode	**$150**	**$150**	**$100**	**$200**	**$500**

Certified QuickBooks ProAdvisors
Hourly Rates Overview

Response	General Book-keeping	Non-Software Business Consulting	Generating Reports	Software Install/Setup	Troubleshooting	Training	On-site Maintenance	Telephone Consulting
Count	292	267	272	282	274	281	264	215
Average	**$60**	**$92**	**$73**	**$83**	**$82**	**$80**	**$81**	**$79**
Low	$15	$25	$15	$25	$25	$25	$25	$15
High	$150	$325	$250	$350	$200	$200	$200	$200
Mode (Most Frequent)	**$50**	**$75**	**$75**	**$75**	**$75**	**$75**	**$75**	**$75**

Fixed Fees Overview

Response	Installation and Setup (New User)	Quarterly Tune-Up	Personal Training (1-2 Hrs.)	Personal Training (3-4 Hrs.)	Personal Training (Full Day)
Count	102	106	106	102	95
Average	**$390**	**$258**	**$162**	**$296**	**$584**
Low	$25	$25	$25	$50	$85
High	$3000	$1200	$540	$550	$1500
Mode	**$250**	$250	$150	$300	$500

All CPAs
Hourly Rates Overview

Response	General Book-keeping	Non-Software Business Consulting	Generating Reports	Software Install/ Setup	Troubleshooting	Training	On-site Mainte-nance	Telephone Consulting
Count	365	355	326	330	335	312	298	265
Average	**$71**	**$114**	**$88**	**$97**	**$98**	**$97**	**$97**	**$97**
Low	$15	$35	$15	$35	$35	$30	$35	$25
High	$180	$275	$250	$350	$250	$265	$250	$265
Mode (Most Frequent)	$50	$100	$75	$75	$75	$75	$75	$75

Fixed Fees Overview

Response	Installation and Setup (New User)	Quarterly Tune-Up	Personal Training (1-2 Hrs.)	Personal Training (3-4 Hrs.)	Personal Training (Full Day)
Count	160	164	138	137	131
Average	**$388**	**$276**	**$181**	**$335**	**$658**
Low	$50	$60	$53	$53	$53
High	$3000	$1200	$540	$600	$1500
Mode	**$250**	$150	$150	$300	$500

153

Originally published in part or in whole in "2007 Intuit Rates Survey," by Bill Teague and Intuit Inc., Intuit® ProConnection® Newsletter, May 2007 (VI:3). © 2007 by Intuit Inc. Used by permission. All rights reserved. The Intuit ProConnection Newsletter is published each month electronically and several times a year to give accounting professionals the information and tools they need to succeed.

Appendix C

Profile of Liz Alexander

Advanced Certified QuickBooks ProAdvisor
Certified QuickBooks Point of Sale ProAdvisor
Member, Intuit Certified Trainer Network
Member, Intuit Accountants Speakers Bureau
Member of the Accountant and Advisor Customer Council of
Intuit Inc., 2006-2007

Elizabeth S. Alexander, CPA
Arlington, TX
817-492-1040 office

Michelle Long: Good afternoon. My name is Michelle Long and I would like to welcome you to "Profiles of Successful QuickBooks Consultants." I would like to go ahead and ask our guest, if you could go and introduce yourself and give us your name and your business and your location.

Liz Alexander: My name is Liz Alexander and I am the owner of Elizabeth Alexander, CPA accounting firm in Arlington, Texas.

Michelle Long: Well. Thanks Liz. I am glad you have taken the time tonight to talk with us. Can you tell us a little bit about your background, both your education and your experience?

Liz Alexander: Sure. I actually have a homegrown degree from here in Arlington, the Bachelors of Business Degree in Accounting from UT (University of Texas) Arlington and I am working on a Master's in Taxation degree. Experience-wise, it goes everywhere from the software industry to the federal government, to telecom, to public accounting. So I pretty much touched a lot of different industries incorporate into the business.

Michelle Long: That is great that you have such a wide range of experience. What prompted you to actually start your own business?

Liz Alexander: Honestly, I wanted to do more stuff with my kids and I never wanted to do another audit as long as I live.

Michelle Long: I can relate to that—I don't want to do taxes. So what year was it that you started your own business?

Liz Alexander: 2003.

Michelle Long: Okay so you started about four years ago.

Liz Alexander: Four years on October 1st.

Michelle Long: Wow. You have an anniversary coming up, that's great. Can you share some of startup experiences, some challenges that you have faced or things that you wish you might have done differently or something that worked really great for you?

Liz Alexander: The biggest challenge I think was some of my colleagues thinking my move was a huge mistake. My biggest mistake was my attempt to purchase some clients from another CPA firm. I found out later (after these clients didn't really materialize and I was out several thousand dollars) that their license is actually suspended. So, that was a hassle that could've been avoided. I ended up getting some of my money back with the help of a lawyer, but it was definitely a learning experience. Never buy somebody else's clients! Another thing that worked though was starting out small. I started working out of my home and didn't move into an office until after two years. And really just by providing the same service that you expect yourself to provide (which is the best possible) you immediately start getting referrals. I started with one client and it was like the old commercial where they "told two friends, and so on, and so on," and then I pretty much had to start turning down business because of all the referrals.

Michelle Long: Wow. That is great.

Liz Alexander: Yeah. It was pretty cool. One really good move (which I didn't realize at the time) was swapping services with a local business directory publisher. She is another woman entrepreneur, and her publication, the Metro Woman Directory, is geared towards women. I've done her accounting, and she's run my ad since almost day one.

Michelle Long: That is great.

Liz Alexander: Yeah. It's been awesome. So finding people who you can swap services with is great.

Michelle Long: That is a great idea. So you have been in business for four years now. How has your business grown and expanded over the years? Have there been any bumps along the way or anything that worked great? I know you mentioned that directory anything else?

Liz Alexander: Yeah. The directory is awesome, and it's been four years. I actually started out planning to work part-time. So this was only supposed to be a part-time gig for me, but it has turned into more than full-time. It's grown to the point where I had to hire another QuickBooks consultant.

Michelle Long: That is good.

Liz Alexander: Yeah. Probably one of the hardest things though is being able to prune that bottom layer of clients that you have to get rid of in order to keep growing.

Michelle Long: Yes that is a hard thing to learn.

Liz Alexander: I think one of the biggest challenges is learning how to let those people go.

Michelle Long: Yes that is hard to learn. There are some clients that you need to let go. That is great that you have done that. So what is your business like today? You mentioned that you have an employee. What type of clients or specialties do you have and what type of services do you offer?

Liz Alexander: After three years and nine months I finally found my first employee. Hiring employees can create growing pains. When you take on that first employee, it's not easy to hand off that first client because nobody does it like you do. So that is how we have grown employee wise. Regarding my clients, they include almost everything across the spectrum. We have retail stores, service industries, wineries, doctors, dentists, and everything in between. I have learned what I don't like to do. I stay away from construction and stay away from manufacturing.

Michelle Long: Great! Liz, do you have a home office or an outside office and what are your thoughts on this topic?

Liz Alexander: For two years my office was in house. Since I didn't want strange people coming into your house, we had a lot of meetings at IHOP with coffee and pancakes. At some point you just get too busy and you want to leave work at the office (or at least try to). So, almost two years ago, I moved into an outside office. With the idea of starting small, I also subleased half of it to another company.

Michelle Long: That was a good idea.

Liz Alexander: Yeah it's great, because I didn't need that much room. I do a lot of work from home on remote desktop or LogMeIn, and it's been great. We've done something a little different with the office. We have an extra room that neither of us is using, so we turned it into kid's room we both have elementary school aged kids. So we have building blocks, art

their entire payroll at a fixed price. It's routine and they know what it is going to cost. Sometimes I lose money; sometimes I make money, but it's starting to take off. I am still pretty much an hourly girl though.

Michelle Long: Yes me too! What type of marketing and networking events do you do or do you attend like the chamber or others. I know you have mentioned something about a local small business assistance center?

Liz Alexander: I am a networking person in that I can talk to anybody. I started out with the Chamber of Commerce because it seemed like the most logical. They had a small business group and would do business over breakfast. That started taking a lot of time and the chamber had some shifts in priorities with incoming and outgoing leaderships. So that's not so much a priority anymore. I do some marketing and networking with the local business assistance center. I don't really get a lot of clients from it, but I get to find out what's on the minds of new entrepreneurs before they start. You find out that bookkeeping isn't a priority for them, but I can at least tell them why they need to at least think about it. And my absolute favorite group is The Joy of Connecting. One of my clients started one of these groups locally.

Michelle Long: And it's called the Joy of what?

Liz Alexander: It's called The Joy of Connecting. I will give you the website. It is http://thejoyofconnecting.com . It's a non-member group, and their mission is to support women entrepreneurs, business owners and other professional women. So, my client started one of these and now there are about 10 of them in the Dallas/Fort Worth area. I don't have a lot of spare of time, but I absolutely love the program and attend as many as I can. It's the coolest thing, because you get to meet women like yourself but who are consumers too.

Michelle Long: So I assume you use that to cultivate and encourage referrals right? Do you have any other marketing tips that work well for you?

Liz Alexander: Absolutely. It depends on your personality. I have never been able to say "please give me five names of your best friends," because I feel like a life insurance salesman and I just can't do it. I talk to my clients about things other than their business. Lots of times, the conversation jogs something in their memory about someone they know who could use our services.

Michelle Long: That's a good way to work it.

Liz Alexander: Yeah. That way you are not really saying "send your friends and neighbors over," but they see that you have knowledge, and it's a bridge into the other part of their life, which is the other people they know.

Michelle Long: That is great. It is something that is working well for you.

Liz Alexander: Yeah. It works really well.

Michelle Long: What are your thoughts on working with or collaborating with other ProAdvisors? Have you done any of these or do you plan on doing it and how that works for you?

Liz Alexander: I wish I knew what everybody else told you about this. I have mixed feelings actually about ProAdvisors specifically.

Michelle Long: Or other accountants.

Liz Alexander: Yes, or other accountants. Some accountants and ProAdvisors tend to be very territorial, and I've had unfortunate experiences locally. I have actually been to training with other ProAdvisors, and the others would not talk to you - they didn't want to get to know you. And they certainly didn't want to tell you anything about themselves, because there was this perceived "I want your business factor" in the room. I wanted to tell them that I have more business than I can handle and that I didn't want theirs...but it was hard and frustrating. So it's been a...

Michelle Long: A challenge.

Liz Alexander: It's been a challenge. That being said, there are groups like the Sleeter group. Through that network, I have met two or three other ProAdvisors who I have talked to on bulletin boards and offline. We have actually sent clients back and forth and email each other our problems, and they are really open.

Michelle Long: Liz, let me ask you a question. Do you think it helps when you are not in same city to be able to collaborate with others?

Liz Alexander: Yes.

Michelle Long: Then it's not as competitive if you are not in the same area?

Liz Alexander: Absolutely. 100%

Michelle Long: Yeah. That is what I have found as well.

Liz Alexander: Yes, because nobody wants to share experiences, and it is frustrating. Another thing about being in the same city that I am finding is that I recognize some of the less qualified ProAdvisors are local CPAs. I am getting their train wrecks and yet still have to be nice and maintain a professional relationship with them...

Michelle Long: Cleaning up after them.

Liz Alexander: Yeah, because I am cleaning up their mess. For instance, I have a client who saw another local CPA who was also a ProAdvisor. They clearly gave my client wrong information which has cost the client about an extra $20,000. Now they're paying me to sweep up the pieces and use a non-QuickBooks program that doesn't do the job as well. So it can be hard to work with people locally. On the other hand, I met a local CPA while at the Sleeter Conference in Las Vegas. She is over in Dallas; I am on the Fort Worth side. She and I hit it off, and she has referred a client to me who has worked out quite well. So it does depend on the personality. I would say it's challenging, but don't use your first experience to judge how every other experience is going to be with other ProAdvisors.

Michelle Long: That is a good observation.

Michelle Long: So what changes do you see coming over the next three to five years for QuickBooks consultants?

Liz Alexander: For QuickBooks consultants specifically, lots of remote computing.

Michelle Long: Yes, Remote Access.

Liz Alexander: Lots of Remote Access and for those of us who do taxes, lots of integration. There is an increasing amount of non-tax integration too with point of sale systems, wireless merchant service terminals, and others that keep you from doing the same work twice.

Michelle Long: Right, more EDI, more integration.

Liz Alexander: Yes, but for the small businesses too. EDI used to be thought of as only relating to larger warehouse manufacturers and "Big Box" types of stores. We are getting to a point now, I think, where the technology is here and the cost is low enough so that even small businesses can now take advantage of it and realize some of the same efficiencies.

Michelle Long: Any other comments, suggestions or words of advice that you would like to include?

164

Liz Alexander: I would say my biggest suggestion is to have a support system in place—even if it's another entrepreneur who isn't your client and you aren't theirs. Just going to get coffee with someone every few weeks to have somebody to talk to helps. Otherwise you are going to drive yourself crazy. I didn't have a support system in place in the beginning, and it made things a lot smoother once I realized I needed that support system. When you go to work for yourself and leave an office environment, you lose your social peer group.

Michelle Long: Yes. It is a big transition.

Liz Alexander: Yes. I wish I had figured that out sooner than later.

Michelle Long: Well, that's a very good piece of advice there. Well great. I want to thank you Liz for taking the time this evening to join us.

Appendix D

Profile of Dawn Scranton

Advanced Certified QuickBooks ProAdvisor
Certified QuickBooks Point of Sale ProAdvisor
Certified QuickBooks Enterprise ProAdvisor
Author of: *QuickBooks Add-ons & Integration Consulting*

Accounting Directors, Inc.
West Palm Beach, FL
www.accountingdirectors.com

Michelle Long: Good morning. My name is Michelle Long and I would like to welcome you to Profiles of Successful QuickBooks Consultants. I would like to ask our guest to go ahead and introduce yourself and give us the name of your business and your location.

Dawn Scranton: Hi, my name is Dawn Scranton from Accounting Directors. I am from the southeast region of Florida.

Michelle Long: Thank you Dawn for joining us this morning. Could you tell us a little bit about your background, education and experiences?

Dawn Scranton: Sure. I have been in the accounting field for approximately 25 years. I began when I was earning my bachelors degree from an entrepreneurial business college. I then worked in the corporate environment educating department managers for almost 10 years when I decided to hang my own shingle about 15 years ago.

Michelle Long: And what prompted you to go ahead and start your own business?

Dawn Scranton: I actually had two motivators. One motivator was my instructors and the corporate supervisors that I was working with. They encouraged me repeatedly suggesting that I was very entrepreneurial and they also suggested that a corporate setting was limiting my potential. And then secondly, while I was in college I worked a lot in part-time bookkeeping jobs working with small business owners. I was trouble shooting everything from general ledger accounts to software applications and even sometimes business procedures or processes. I really loved working with small business and mom and pop type organizations and having a chance to see results of the recommendations I was putting in place.

Michelle Long: So, it sounds like you have both education and a lot of hands on experience before you went on your own. Do you want to share any of your startup experiences, as you were getting started? Any challenges you faced or things you wish you would have done differently or anything that maybe worked out really great for you?

Dawn Scranton: When I started I found that finding clients was actually very easy, if the state offers a listing of everyone that applies for an occupational license. So, I started from there and drafted a letter advertising bookkeeping services. But as I continued to grow I found that managing growth was the biggest challenge that I still continued to face everyday, even now. Even after experience with working with other business owners and experience with working in a corporate environment. I still find that my own housekeeping, that is staffing concerns, internal and external communications and time management continue to burn a lot more energy than I ever anticipated. What I probably should have done differently was hire more business coaches and consultants that could help me with some of my learning deficits, for example recruiters, marketing consultants and web designers.

Michelle Long: That's a good point—to hire some people to help you with managing your own business.

Dawn Scranton: Correct. I was trying to do everything myself. I am guilty of the same thing that I accuse my clients of – You cannot go shopping at Home Depot and then call yourself a General Contractor. Sometimes we catch ourselves making the same mistake. The more you try to do-it-yourself, the more you allow other management tasks to go unmanaged.

Michelle Long: Right. So realizing that you need help as well?

Dawn Scranton: Exactly.

Michelle Long: What is your business like to date? Do you use employee or subcontractors or what type of clients do you have in? Tell us about your specialties and services you offer.

Dawn Scranton: Well we started out assisting Quick-Books users back in the beginning. So that's been since 1993, almost 15 years. Although we began as part-time bookkeepers, we quickly grew into mini-controller type services. Then most recently we moved into system integration consultants as we taught our clients to become more automated. What we have learned was the result of our clients challenging us to seek out integrated solutions that eliminated duplicate data entry. So, as they grew we grew with them. In 2003, we gave up the book-keeping and tax practices and started focusing solely on IDN (Intuit Developer Network) solutions and opportunities. This allowed us to triple our revenue while this alleviating our staffing needs. One of our challenges today is that this type of work spikes and falls rapidly. So, sometimes we wish it was a little more level. That's where we find our relationships with our developers and ProAdvisors are extremely valuable as well as our business coaches. We can rely on them for these ups and downs that we are experiencing and sometimes level them a little bit. So, we have been focusing a lot on working with out-sourced staffing. We work with three different developing companies that have different expertise. Sometimes we find that some have strength in SQL while others have strength in MS Access. So it depends on the project as to who we outsource to. That became crucial for me to be able to form relationships with people that I could trust. And we have had the same experience with ProAdvisors, where sometimes they are advanced and they can handle trouble shooting much faster than someone who is new that is much stronger with just data-entry.

Michelle Long: OK. So some of it sounds like it's been trial and error in identifying the people that you wanted to partner within to work with?

Dawn Scranton: Absolutely.

Michelle Long: So you let some of the developers handle their strength, while you handle some of the integration aspects with QuickBooks. Is that correct?

Dawn Scranton: Yes. We have become project manager leaders while we try to use our outsourced relationships to keep the ball rolling and to keep the project in progress.

Michelle Long: Wow. You said tripled your revenue once you started specializing?

Dawn Scranton: Yes, we originally started out doing a lot of data-entry and general ledger reconciliation, which is valued at a much lower rate. We found that by helping businesses pull data from different sources while eliminating the duplication of data entry, clients were willing to pay three times the rate (on an hourly basis) than what they were willing to pay for the data entry.

Michelle Long: Because you are helping them to make it more efficient, save them time.

Dawn Scranton: Money and time. For all the times we eliminate a person's job or part-time bookkeeping jobs and we are able to save them $30,000 in their first year after our first two or three consultations. So, to them there is a lot of value in that and that allows me to write my own ticket from my invoicing.

Michelle Long: Wow. It sounds like you found a great specialty. Are you working from home or did you ever have a home office? Did you move to an outside office or what are your thoughts on that matter?

Dawn Scranton: I am working from a home office. I am looking right now to relocate to a commercial space. I have bounced that idea back and forth a 1,000 times. In the beginning when we were doing bookkeeping, I didn't need it because we were traveling bookkeepers and we would go to the businesses location. The only time I needed a professional space was for a conference, and I found that I could do that through other avenues. More recently though, with project planning, a lot of times I need a space, so I can bring together a group of professionals and that puts a different spin on things. Now my clients are looking for a professional consultant that can communicate with other professional consultants. There is a prestigious image that comes with that. Unfortunately, one of the things that really aggravates me – is that business owners assume when you work from home, that a Futon and laptop is what makes up your office furniture.

Michelle Long: Yes, they don't realize that you may have a separate office that is every bit as professional as an outside office.

Dawn Scranton: You have to respect that perception is reality.

Michelle Long: Yes.

Dawn Scranton: And that's where the professional space becomes a lot more valuable.

Michelle Long: OK. So for several years you did have a home office. I can see where you would be working and having meetings with several different consultants and would need some conference room space. So you haven't actually found your outside office yet but you are in the process?

Dawn Scranton: We are looking. Yes.

Michelle Long: So what's your typical week like. How many hours are you working and how much are you networking and tell us little bit about what your week is like?

Dawn Scranton: I personally spent about 25 hours of my week as billable time. I spend another 25 hours a week either managing people and projects or software education or marketing. I am trying to play multiple roles here. I guess this is what most business owners do. Then I have a full time staff person that helps me with marketing and managing of the projects as well. So that's what my typical week looks like.

Michelle Long: I think a lot of people don't realize how much time it really takes for all the non-billable things like maintaining your expertise and managing your own business like you said. What are your thoughts on billing? On billing by the hour versus fix fee?

Dawn Scranton: We use project pricing for two reasons. One we find that clients are looking to know that there is a budget in place or that their expenses are controllable to a certain degree. They also wanted to know what results they can expect at the end of a certain milestone. So, I can give project pricing by phases. I can take one project divide it up into phases and say "look at phase one. This is how much you are going to spend and this is the results you can expect. Then at phase two, we will get this milestone and at phase three, we should have this other objective accomplished." That allows them to mange their finances a little bit better. Another reason we do the project pricing is that we found it demonstrates that we have enough experience to know that what we are doing. We know from doing this in the past, how long this is going to take.

Sometimes when I try to give an hourly rate, it just doesn't seem feasible. When I tried to quote a project on an hourly rate my clients get hesitant and they are like "oh if you have done this before you should know how many hours it's going to take" and I see them fidgeting in their chair. So we find that the project pricing just works better all the way around.

Michelle Long: Do you have a clause or any contingencies for unforeseen events or unexpected complications that might come up that allows you to increase your price?

Dawn Scranton: We do have provisions for things that might fall outside the scope and that's where setting the milestone of what's going to be accomplished at certain points becomes crucial. That's what we create examples, so we can demonstrate what we expect to accomplish. If you want to modify the transaction to include more or less information then we have to account for that variance separately.

Michelle Long: What type of marketing and networking events do you attend and which ones do you find that are the most effective for you?

Dawn Scranton: We highly recommend BNI (Business Networking International) that help develop and test several (what I call) elevator speeches. Here at BNI, they give you 30 seconds to standup and introduce yourself and give a quick commercial and they do that every week. So, that's an opportunity to every week try something different or try the same one and see what the reactions in the room are. So you get a chance to throw out your elevator speech to 30 to 50 people and see what their eyes look like and how they react to it. Whether it's a good fit or bad fit? Or whether they understand what you are trying to say or not. Then we also do a lot of volunteer work. We volunteer for continuing education program through SBA and through the Florida Women Business Center and through the college where I graduated from as well.

Michelle Long: So do you conduct seminars or meet with people one-on-one for the volunteer work?

Dawn Scranton: The volunteer work is usually like a committee type for the college. I am on the committee of continuing education where they will be creating a new continuing education program. For the Florida Women's Business Center, we are doing training on QuickBooks.

Michelle Long: I would imagine that would lead to some networking too with some of the participants in those seminars.

Dawn Scranton: I am in a situation where I can benefit from existing programs and then also create my own.

Michelle Long: So how do you cultivate and encourage referrals and do you have any other marketing tips that have worked really or marketing ideas that you have tried and more over wasted your time and money?

Dawn Scranton: Finding a marketing consultant has proven to be a very big challenge for us. I have hired two or three marketing consulting firms that really didn't understand the methods that I wanted to deliver and didn't understand how to target the clients I was looking for. So, I felt that - unfortunately I wasted a lot of money in that area. What I found did work better was working with business consultants or networking with business management consultants and computer consultants. They have proven to be invaluable. Business management consultants will typically try to show a business owner how to bid a project or how to make their staff accountable and in the course of that line of work, they discover that there are deficiencies in the system. Then they start looking at their data structure and how they are sharing information from out in the field back into the back-office. That is where my value comes in, as they see me as a person that connects the dots from one place to another. The computer consultants see the same thing. They are installing hardware trying to keep up with the business owner's demands for speed and processors and they also see the same pains of lack of integration. So, both of these types of consultants have been extremely valuable to us and much more than any marketing consultants has been able to help us.

Michelle Long: You've really created a network of personal referrals that sounds like it is really working.

Dawn Scranton: Yes.

Michelle Long: You mentioned that you work with some other ProAdvisors. How do you collaborate with other ProAdvisors and how well has that worked? You said you had some that weren't so good. Can you share some of that with us?

Dawn Scranton: Yeah. We find that there are a lot of ProAdvisors that prefer to work from home remotely and just want to get their hours in and then be done with the project. That is okay for some types of projects. Then we find there are other ProAdvisors that are much more advanced. They want to do trouble shooting. They want to do technology implementation. So one of the things that we have done is we have created an association called the Association of QuickBooks Technologists. We are using that association to find ProAdvisors that are passed their fifth year as QuickBooks consultants that are looking for work that is more challenging than data entry work. We still relay on the ProAdvisors that are more geared to data entry work, because though they become our backbone. They become the ProAdvisor that can help us get caught up on a large project. When we are doing an implementation of software and the client will say, "Help me fix my exiting database, so that we can prepare for the integrated solution." For example, we were doing an event yesterday for government contractors and the chart of accounts for government contractors has to be setup in a specific fashion so that the government contracting add-on software can work effectively. So, a ProAdvisor that specializes in data entry can sometime restructure the chart of accounts for us or they can make sure that the data that is getting entered is entered in a format that meets what the add-on is going to need.

Michelle Long: So you use them as subcontractors on your job. That helps you to get the help that you need sot that you can work at a higher level. That is a great way to set it up. What are the changes you see coming for QuickBooks Consultants over the next three to five years?

Dawn Scranton: I see a lot of business to business integration that is gaining in popularity right now. In other words data entry is being eliminated. Let me give you an example. I was reading an article the other day that says "email is used 80% of the time for processing an order." So you can imagine that when someone gets an email that says "I would like to order your product." Someone has to take that email manually and enter it into another system. So, there are a lot of system integration consultants right now that are focusing on, how do we take that email and get it into a system without human intervention and you don't see a lot of that occurring. I am now communicating with two or three developers outside the U.S. that are looking at that exact example of how we can transfer information from one business to another. For example, if I was setting up a QuickBooks invoice today and I send it out to my supplier. My supplier should be able to receive the invoice via email and then also import it into his own QuickBooks file or his own accounting application. We are going to see a lot more of that occurring in the next two years or three years. There is a big focus on that out there right now. If you can communicate with all your suppliers and customers through an interface that pulls your transactions directly into their database there will be a lot of elimination of data entry.

Michelle Long: This leads back to the discussion about the amount of non-billable time that is spent trying to stay proficient with all the changes and new things. It takes time to stay on top of that doesn't it?

176

Dawn Scranton: Absolutely. People are astonished when I tell them that I try to learn one or two new software applications every month and they say "wow that's a lot of software." I do it because that is what I have to do to stay on top of the market place. That is what I have to do to understand what is available for the client and how I can benefit from the technology that's coming up.

Michelle Long: Because things are changing so fast, you have to be continuously learning and staying on top of it. Well Dawn, do you have any other comments or suggestion or any other words of advice for other consultants that you would like to let us share with us?

Dawn Scranton: Well, there is one more thing I would like to remind ProAdvisors or anyone that's listening is to keep in mind that you have to encourage your clients to embrace automation, because you have taught them how to use QuickBooks. This means that you have unknowingly embedded the idea of embracing new technology and while you taught them how to use QuickBooks don't forget to ask yourself what have you done lately that is embracing new technology? Are you walking into their office with a PDA device and showing them how to invoice from a PDA while you are on the job site or you still doing it manually? Because what you are doing says a lot about who you are.

Michelle Long: That is great advice—to set an example by staying on top of technology ourselves.

Dawn Scranton: Exactly.

Michelle Long: Well Dawn, I really appreciate you taking the time to join us this morning.

Dawn Scranton: Thank you

Appendix E

Resources

Author: mlong@mlongconsulting.com – Please send me your comments and suggestions for the next edition!

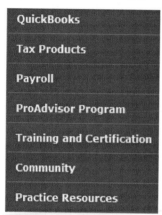

Accountant.intuit.com – This website is the gateway to a wealth of free information for accountants and QuickBooks consultants. The sections for Quickbooks, Tax Products, and Payroll provide details about Intuit's complete family of products and services. The following menus are all within accountant.intuit.com.

Under ProAdvisor Program you will find all the details about the program and its benefits and resources available.

Training and Certification

> QuickBooks and Payroll Training

Lacerte Training

ProSeries Training

QuickBooks Certification

Advanced QuickBooks Certification

Point of Sale Certification

Enterprise Solutions Certification

Intuit Education Program

Community

Practice Resources

Within the Training and Certification section you can improve your knowledge base via seminars, webinars, webcasts, or self-study courses. This is where you will find the certification information and course lockers.

Community

Forums

Community Resource Library

Find Local ProAdvisor

Help

Practice Resources

The Community section is also a resource for improving your knowledge base, researching issues, as well as connecting with your peers.

Practice Resources

Seminar Resources

Intuit ProConnection

Test drives, trials, brochures, and kits

Product Tips

Tax Resource Center

Comparison Charts

Access Your Peers

Helpful Links

Within the Practice Resources section you will find the Intuit ProConnection tab which is discussed below. Under Seminar Resources, there are numerous resources and tools (from the various seminars for accountants) available for downloading.

Practice Resources

Seminar Resources

> Intuit ProConnection

   Current Newsletter

   Enroll

   Subscriber Center

   > Archive

   FAQs

   Resources

   Troubleshooting

   Articles

Test drives, trials, brochures, and kits

Product Tips

Tax Resource Center

Comparison Charts

Access Your Peers

Helpful Links

Many tools, sample engagement letters, checklists, and Intuit's **Annual Rates Survey** can be found within the Intuit ProConnection section within the articles. You should definitely enroll to get the newsletter. Spend some time exploring all the resources available that cover a variety of topics such as marketing, product tips and more.

ProAdvisor Website

When you join the ProAdvisor Program, you will have access to **www.qbadvisor.com**. Here you will find even more information to help increase your knowledge base, grow you practice, train, and save. Again, there is a wealth of free information, resources and tools for downloading. Within the Train the Trainer section you will find every thing you need to conduct Quick-Books classes or seminars including instructor notes, presentation slides, and student handouts. There is course material for the following courses: QuickBooks Pro, Quick-Books Point of Sale, QuickBooks Premier for Contractors, and Simple Start.

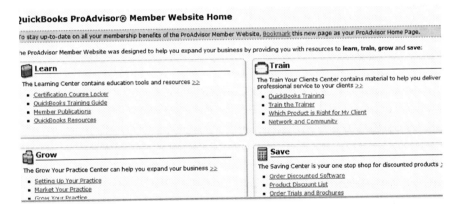

Marketplace.intuit.com

This is an online resource of third-party add-on integration applications that work with QuickBooks.

The resources noted below are provided for informational purposes only to assist you with further research. This is not an endorsement or guarantee of their product or service. You should do your own research and make your own decisions as to which vendors to use.

Business Cards:

www.overnightprints.com or www.vistaprints.com or a variety of other online printing companies.

Website Hosting: (and domain name availability)

GoDaddy, Network Solutions, Netfirms, Yahoo, Homestead, among numerous other web hosting companies.

If you join the ProAdvisor Program, you are entitled to a three page website from Homestead for twelve months.

Incorporation Services:

Intuit's www.MyCorporation.com or numerous other companies

Other Resources for starting and growing your business:

Agencies and Organizations that may provide counseling, seminars, and resources include:

> Small Business Development Centers (SBDC) –
>> available in every state – go to www.asbdc-us.org
> Women's Business Centers (WBC)
> SCORE (Service Corps of Retired Executives)

There are numerous organizations available for assistance. You must take the initiative to seek out the resources in your area.